Writing Matters
2005-2006

The University of
North Carolina at Greensboro

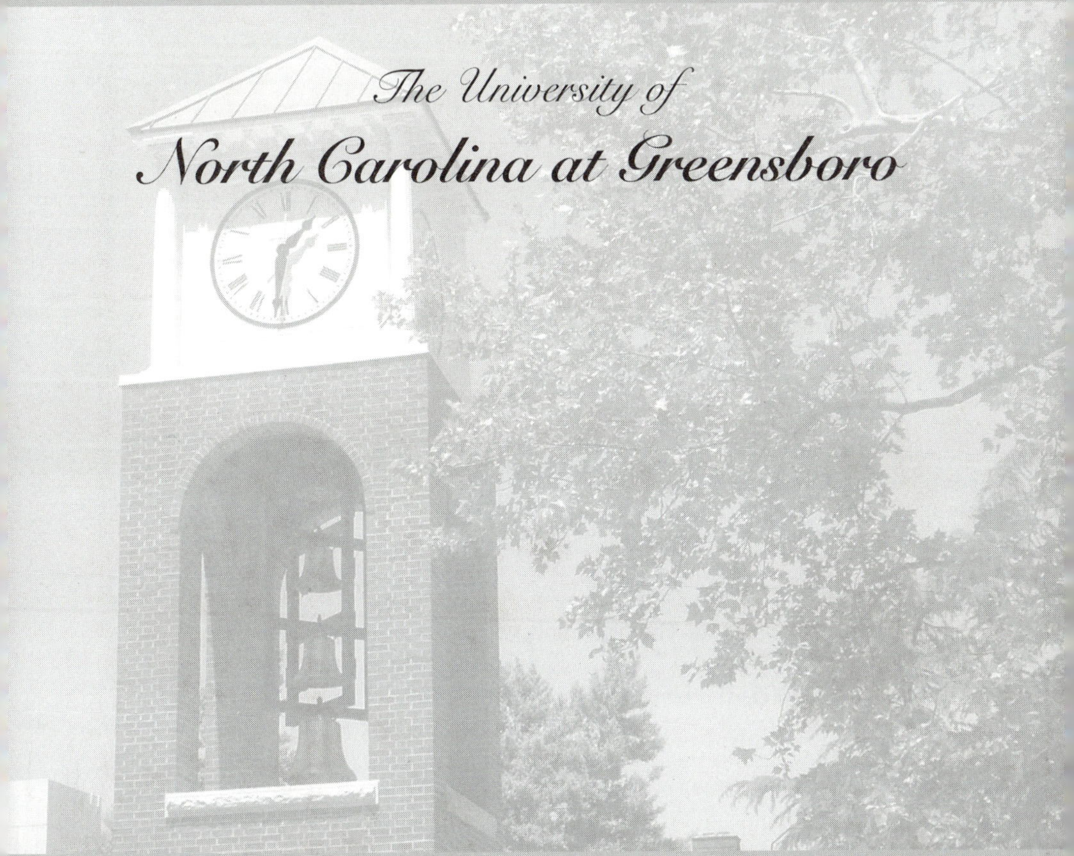

Edited by
Rita Jones-Hyde, Karen C. Summers
and Liz Vogel

KENDALL/HUNT PUBLISHING COMPANY
4050 Westmark Drive　　Dubuque, Iowa 52002

Cover image courtesy of The University of North Carolina-Greensboro

Copyright © 2005, The University of North Carolina-Greensboro

ISBN 0-7575-2156-8

Kendall/Hunt Publishing Company has the exclusive rights to reproduce this work, to prepare derivative works from this work, to publicly distribute this work, to publicly perform this work and to publicly display this work.

All rights reserved. No part of this publication may be reproduced, stored in a retrieval system, or transmitted, in any form or by any means, electronic, mechanical, photocopying, recording, or otherwise, without the prior written permission of the copyright owner.

Printed in the United States of America

10 9 8 7 6 5 4 3 2

Contents

Acknowledgments	vii
The Writing Matters Legacy	ix
From the Composition Director	xi

Rhetoric! Huh. What Is It Good For? — 1

English 101: A Primer *Hephzibah Roskelly*	3
Rhetoric! Huh. What Is It Good For? *Rod Spellman*	7
Visual Rhetoric in the Composition Classroom *Allison Cooper*	11
Theory into Practice: Visual Rhetoric *"Big Fishes: A Testimony to Life"* *Daniel Stine*	13
Revision: Take Two, Take Three *Liz Vogel*	15

All You Ever Wanted to Know about 101 (But Were Too Afraid to Ask) — 17

Reading Actively — 19
Laura Savu

Theory into Practice: Reading Actively "Japanese Internment" — 23
Michael Rawls

Why Are the Readings Such a Pain? A Case for Complexity and Critical Theory — 27
Sara Littlejohn

So Happy Together: Making the Most of Group Assignments — 29
Robert Brandon

Workin' It: Workshops in the Classroom — 32
David Rogers

The Portfolio: Watch It Develop — 35
Todd Atchison

English Composition Portfolio Contest — 37

All Freshman Read — 38

"Can Someone Please Help Me Find My Voice?": Speaking in the Composition Classroom — 39
Michelle Johnson

Words that Start with "S" — 42
G. Warlock Vance

Student-Teacher Conferencing — 44
Karen C. Summers

Literature in the Writing Classroom — 46
Lee Templeton

"You Want Me to Do What?": Assignments in the Composition Classroom — 49

Journaling 101 — 51
Rita Jones-Hyde

Writing the Reflective Essay — 54
Laura Alexander

Creative Writing in the Composition Classroom — 56
Joe Wagner

Theory Into Practice: Creative Writing *"A Buñuelian Experience"* — 58
Ben Barbour

Interpreting Our World: An Introduction to Ethnography — 60
Janet White

Theory into Practice: Ethnography *"The Club Hoppers & the Rabbits Outside"* — 62
Ashley Jones

Stage Fright—Minus the Stage — 65
Tamara Wiandt

A Rookie's Guide to Research — 68
Temeka L. Carter

Theory into Practice: Research Papers *"Psycho: A Film Score Analysis"* — 71
Nick Melton

Surviving College Writing: Don't Be the First One Kicked Off the Island — 75

Academic Integrity — 77
Aaron Chandler

The Writing Center — 78
Liz Wilkinson

Other UNCG English Courses — 81

Campus and Web Resources — 83

Contest Winners — 87

"In the Shadows" — 89
Katherine D. Frazier

"A Long Time Ago, in a Starbucks Far, Far Away . . ." — 94
Darrin Powell

"I'm (the) Only Me" — 97
James Houghton

"White Bullies" — 100
James Houghton

Writing Matters Submission Form — 107

Acknowledgments

Copy Editors
Michelle Johnson
Rod Spellman
Sara Littlejohn
Jennifer Whitaker

Writing Contest Winner
Katherine Frazier

Finalists
Darrin Powell
James Houghton

Writing Contest Student Judges
Matt Allor
Rob Pantell
Kini Johnson
Justin Hall
John Whitfield
Steven Pericht
Linda Tan
Alison Friday

Writing Contest Committee
Laura Alexander
Sandy Hartwiger
Sara Littlejohn

Special Thanks: Hephzibah Roskelly, Elizabeth Chiseri-Strater, Lydia Howard, Stephen Yarbrough, Dr. Heidi Hanrahan, and the students who contributed essays and the instructors who encouraged them.

The Writing Matters Legacy

For the past nine years, graduate students from the UNCG English department have edited, contributed and constructed a comprehensive guide for English 101 students. These graduate students have drawn from their own experiences in the classroom as well as from the thoughts of their students. Without the former efforts of our fellow peers and the hard work of our students, *Writing Matters* would not be what it is today. We, the editors, would like to thank those that have come before us. Thank you to all that have worked with *Writing Matters* and with *Write Angles*.

Diann L. Baecker
Janet Bean
David Carithers
Timothy Flood
Keith Gammons
Jackie Grutsch McKinney
Bob Haas
Heidi Hanrahan
Beth Howells
Rebecca Jones

Kay McEvoy
Jewel Mayberry
Cynthia Nearman
Bethany Perkins
Chris Porter
Warren Rochelle
Katie Ryan
Judit Szerdahelyi
Lee Torda
Jason Tower

From the Composition Director

Welcome to the Composition Program at UNCG. I hope you will have a successful experience in your first college English course and that you'll be excited about what you'll do in English 101. The English Department considers this course to be one of the most important you'll ever take and expects that you will find it challenging, fun, and thoughtful. There are many things about this course that will be familiar to you from your own high school English classes, but we know there are some practices and ideas you'll find different. The purpose of this guide is to introduce you to some of the beliefs about writing and learning shared by the instructors who teach in this composition program.

The most important thing to know about English 101 is that it is a writing course. It is designed to help you gain practice in completing a variety of writing tasks, to improve your understanding of your own writing process, and to learn how reading and writing are intimately connected. In this course you will learn how to investigate ideas, data, and sources in ways that will help you in your college career, but more importantly, in ways that will lead you to understand what you think about important ideas about yourself as well.

This program is guided by some shared assumptions about writing you may want to know:

- All writers have a process, or procedure, in composing.
- Making that process conscious is a way to understand it better.
- All students have the potential to write powerful prose because all writers use language in their everyday lives.
- Writers learn from one another.

- Writers do better work when they are engaged and invested in their writing topics.
- Writing frequently, both formally and informally, leads to writing better.
- Writers are made, not born.

Classroom practices in English 101 support and extend these ideas. Some of the writing you do will be reflective in an attempt to get you to think about your own process of composing and revising. Some writing will ask you to analyze the ideas you discover in reading and in research. Some will encourage you to develop arguments or support contentions and beliefs you have. Often you will write in ungraded and informal ways to help you practice forms and ideas. Journaling, scrapbooks, letters, short notes, and commentaries are important forms of writing for this course.

By the end of this course, you will have written twenty or more pages of revised prose, and you will assemble your work into a portfolio for evaluation. Grades are not usually given on individual papers; instead, your writing will be considered as a whole. You and your instructor will conference at midterm and at the end of the semester. This approach to grading may be different from what you are used to, but we hope you'll find this approach a way of freeing yourself from being overly concerned with grades. We want you to be more concerned with the real work of a writing course, which is content and style—with what you have to say and how you say it.

This book has been written by experienced instructors who teach in our writing program and is aimed entirely at you. English 101 is the only required course for all Freshman students (although later you will take four Writing Intensive courses), and we want you to be successful in this course and in your college career. We hope this guide will help you do just that. In the following pages we discuss the philosophy of our program, its shared practices and beliefs, and the resources that are available to you.

This book contains our philosophy of reading and writing: we describe what rhetoric is and how it guides and shapes our composition program. We talk about reading in the writing course and how becoming a good reader will help you become a better writer. We describe approaches that are common in our program: journals, writing conferences, portfolios, and collaborative group work—all practices that reflect the expectations of you as a reader, writer, and learner in English 101. Group work, for example, demands that you work closely with others, assume responsibility for your contributions to the group, and allow yourself to learn new perspectives and ideas from collaborating with your group as you share your writing.

There are many resources available to you as a student in English 101, and we want you to know about them. If English is not your first language, you'll want to know that we offer courses that may meet your needs: English 101N is for non-native speakers, and English 203 is a course that introduces students to college life. All students at UNCG are encouraged to use the resources of the Writing Center, located in 101 McIver, which offers free tutoring in writing across the disciplines. Additionally, you may take English 102S, a speaking intensive course taught by many of the same instructors who teach 101. If so, you will find the resources available in the Speaking Center, located in 22 McIver, helpful for you. The Jackson Library is another resource that all students at UNCG, particularly first-year students, should take advantage of when doing research in writing courses.

I hope you'll find this book about our first-year program a helpful guide for your English 101 course as well as for other writing courses you will take in your years here at UNCG.

Rhetoric! Huh. What Is It Good For?

English 101: A Primer

Hephzibah Roskelly

Beliefs

There are as many ways to write as there are writers perhaps, and there are just as many ideas about how writing happens best. But your composition class is guided by some ideas about how to write and how to write most effectively that are helpful for you to know:

- Every writer has a process.
- Making that process conscious is a way to intervene in it and/or support it.
- Every writer has the potential to produce powerful prose because every writer is a language user.
- Writers learn from one another.
- Writing tasks need to have meaning for the writer to be successful.
- Writing a lot leads to writing better.

Writing Is a Process

Every writer has a process even if it's mostly unconscious. We all come up with ideas, think about them, get them down on paper, alter them and complete whatever it is we're working on, often by giving it to someone else. Part of the work of your composition class is to help you make the process you use more conscious, and so that you will make better writing choices. Do you wait a long time to begin a piece of writing? Do you spend so much time changing a sentence that you don't have time to look at the whole paragraph? Do you write quickly or slowly? Do you like to have somebody to talk to about your ideas? Knowing how you write and how you write best is the first step to becoming more confident and effective as a writer.

You probably are familiar with the steps of a typical writing process:

- **Invention**—how you gather ideas, formulate positions, consider possibilities: Reading, writing, talking, making notes, finding quotes, are all invention activities.
- **Drafting**—how you write from start to finish: on a computer, by hand, with stops and starts, straight through, on different kinds of paper, with notes attached or a host of other techniques
- **Revision**—how you decide to make changes: from the beginning, to paragraphs or ideas, to lengthen or omit, to add proofs or stories, to alter tone.
- **Editing**—how you correct your prose to make it communicate more effectively and efficiently: spelling, word choices, sentence lengths and styles, punctuation, paragraphing.

But it's likely that you don't always engage in all of these processes or with the same amount of attention. If you know that your reader cares mostly about ideas or that what you're writing is supposed to be a draft, you'll likely edit little if at all. If you are submitting a piece of writing for publishing consideration, you'll spend much time revising and editing to convey your sense of serious purpose and skill.

Every decision you make as a writer, in fact, is dependent on purpose, on why you're writing, who's reading, and what you're trying to say. You make decisions about what to leave alone and what to change, when to begin revising, how to choose words, how to use sources, and every other decision based on your aim for your writing piece.

Writers Learn From One Another

We know that most of the knowledge we acquire comes by way of indirection: socially, anecdotally, and because we need it for practical work. Writers learn from others about themselves; as they listen to other writers and to people outside the classroom, they get a clearer sense of themselves, of what they think and know. The group work you do in class helps foster that process.

There is nothing you can do in a composition classroom any more important than group work. Group work allows your voice to be heard in a classroom that is often mostly dominated by only one voice, the teacher's. Voice—hearing it, using it, modulating it—is what good writing is all about, and practice using it in your small group will reap benefits for you as a writer. You will also learn to be more confident as a speaker, and you'll acquire new experience as you listen to diverse experiences and ideas from your fellow group members. You'll also discover how your writing changes as you discuss it with others and get their responses to your written work.

But group work beneficial as it is, is sometimes difficult to do well—or at all—for a host of reasons. None of us is well trained in sharing. We have been taught to do our work—especially our writing—individually, and in some cases have been penalized for letting somebody else "look on" or "help out" as we produced work.

Good group work is not busy work, but a real, organic part of your work as a writer in your composition course. As you share ideas, revise your thinking, pose and solve problems together, you and your group learn to take responsibility and to learn how to explain more effectively and listen more attentively. In the world outside of the university, group work is the way most work gets done, and so your work as a group member is a good preparation for your post college life as well.

Rhetoric in the Writing Class

You may be familiar with the word *rhetoric* but may not know much beyond that it has something to do with language and persuasion. But you're already an expert at using rhetoric. We are all rhetoricians because we all use language to try to communicate ideas and persuade listeners to our point of view. You need to write home for money because you've used your allowance with two weeks still to go before it arrives again. What do you say? You apply for a job at a restaurant that has asked for experienced wait staff, and you've never waited tables before. How do you make yourself sound appealing?

These kinds of situations present themselves to us every day, and we learn how to confront them by using rhetoric. Aristotle's definition of the term, "Rhetoric is the art of observing, in any given case, the available means of persuasion," suggests that people use their experience as humans to locate the ways they might be most convincing to others. Will your mother be persuaded by an appeal to her sympathy for your lack of budgeting? Will the restaurant manager be impressed by your terrific math grades? A rhetorician observes and uses that knowledge to make decisions about what to say and when to say it.

Your writing class will present you with a variety of rhetorical situations in the assignments and activities it offers, and the strategies you choose to accomplish your work will depend on your growing understanding about what might be effective and useful for your readers and for your purpose. Some of the kinds of tasks you might accomplish this semester include:

- a story of experience: a narrative of your own, true or fictional
- an observation of others: a depiction of a group or case study of an individual
- a review; an analysis of a piece of writing or a visual text
- an opinion piece: an argument on an issue
- a researched essay: an argument or exploration of idea that asks for others' opinions or data to be included
- a poem, a short story, a dramatic monologue: an exploration of form

Aristotle's triad, the graphic representation of how the contexts of reader, writer and subject shape writing, is a useful tool to use to study the texts you write and read. How do writer and reader connect? What does a reader need to know or a writer need to demonstrate in order for purpose to be accomplished? How much or how little evidence needs to be cited for readers to be convinced about a subject? How much does a writer reveal about personal background or personal opinion in order to connect with an audience or certify competence? All these questions, and others like them, are the strategies of inquiry you can use effectively to analyze literature, to assess arguments, to form opinions, as well as to write effectively and authoritatively on your own.

Practice with rhetorical analysis can give you a key to unlocking the door of assignments in much of the work you'll be asked to do in college in fact, for you to learn the importance of what Ann Berthoff calls "reading in," understanding the contexts in which writing—even the writing of assignments—occurs.

Rhetoric! Huh. What Is It Good For?

Rod Spellman

Absolutely everything. Well, not quite, but rhetoric is a part of just about every attempt we make at communicating with other people. Chances are, you've only heard about rhetoric in negative terms. The media often talks about "conservative (or liberal) rhetoric," and talk-show announcers dismiss the ideas of people they don't like with comments like, "That's just rhetoric." What these negative comments often mean is that someone is just talking about a problem instead of acting to solve it. However, rhetoric can be a powerful tool in getting problems solved.

Rhetoric is deliberate and effective communication.

Sounds simple, huh? Well, it is, but there is a bit more to it than this simple definition. Let's start with a little time travel . . .

In Ancient Greece, philosophers developed rules for rhetoric that helped them to persuade their fellow citizens. The Greeks did most of their political and legal debating by giving speeches, whereas politicians and lawyers today generally write briefs to explain their positions. As the Greeks got more accomplished at giving speeches, they started to notice what was important and what was unimportant in convincing other people to agree with them. These observations led to the development of a system of rhetoric. Aristotle created what is called the *rhetorical triangle* that summed up the three main components of all communication.

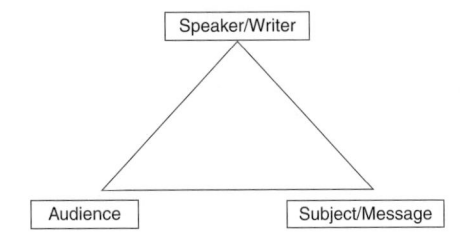

```
         Speaker/Writer
              /\
             /  \
            /    \
           /      \
          /        \
    Audience    Subject/Message
```

These three components are interrelated—changing one affects the others. For example, look back at the title of this section. One of the assumptions I (the writer) am making about you (the audience) is that you will recognize my title (message) as a play on the words to Edwin Starr's song "War." ("War! Huuh. What is it good for? Absolutely nothing.") I can make this assumption with some degree of certainty because I hear this song every few days on the radio, and I guess that you've heard it, as well. If enough of you don't get the reference, then I might need to think some more about my audience. Maybe you're too young to get the reference, and I should think about using lyrics from Pink or Eminem. Or maybe you're too old, and Ella Fitzgerald might be a better choice. In either case, I might have to modify my message to make you understand it better. Understanding the way the three points of the triangle are connected means you are able to communicate more effectively.

To make the triangle more personal to you, think about how you might tell the following people that you had just found the love of your life, and you were running away to get married:

1. Your best friend
2. Your parents
3. Your professor

Would you include the same details in all three conversations? Would you use the same sense of excitement with your parents (who happen to hate your significant other) as with your best friend? Would you just be informing some people, while trying to persuade others? What if you were telling these people that you just passed your hardest class with an A? Notice how changing the message or the audience changes the way you (the speaker/writer) present your ideas. TA DAH! Rhetoric in action!

Those wise old Greek guys went a little bit further, though. They also named some tools for using rhetoric effectively. They decided that most persuasive attempts use one or more of three basic appeals: logos, pathos, and ethos.

Logos attempts to persuade your audience through logic.
Pathos attempts to persuade your audience through emotion.
Ethos attempts to persuade your audience through a sense of ethics.

For example, imagine that you are trying to convince your professor at the end of the semester that you should have a higher grade. If you were making an appeal based on logos, you might try convincing her by statistics: you attended forty-two out of forty-five classes, or you turned in 75% of the homework. A pathos appeal might try to convince her to feel sorry for you: you'll lose your scholarship if you don't get an A, or you wouldn't have missed so many classes if it hadn't been for your sick relative. Ethos appeals usually involve creating a persuasive persona. This persona is the face you show to your audience in order to get them to agree with you. With your professor, you might try convincing her you deserve a good grade because you are a fine, upstanding citizen who helps out in the community, and a bad grade might affect your ability to do community service, or you might say that you are a fellow English major, and English folks ought to help each other out. (I offer you this warning, however. Your professors are already skilled in rhetoric, and they won't be fooled by such persuasive attempts. Your best bet is to use an ethos appeal from the first day of class, one that shows, through your actions, that you are a dependable, intelligent, dedicated, and hard-working individual. Then you don't need to worry about persuasive appeals at the end of the semester!)

Rhetoric is a tool that helps you, as a writer, to determine what and how you write depending on your purpose and audience. However, it also helps you, as a reader, to understand why and how other authors wrote their texts. Keeping the rhetorical triangle in mind as you read helps you to have a clearer picture of what an author is saying, and remembering the types of persuasive appeals helps you to realize when an author is trying to change your mind.

I leave you with a few helpful thoughts about rhetoric in the writing classroom:

- When writing an essay, always keep your audience in mind.
    - How much do they already know about the subject?
    - How much background information will they need?
    - What kind of rhetorical appeals will sway them the most?
    - Will they accept personal stories as evidence, or do they only want facts?
- When writing an essay, think about how you want to be seen by the audience.
    - Are you the wise authority providing information?
    - Are you the friend providing advice?
    - What evidence of your own ability/knowledge do you need to demonstrate to have your audience accept you as a reliable source?

- Do you want to be humorous or serious? (Note that this is also often determined by your subject. A movie review might be quite funny, but we would probably be disturbed by a funny essay about world hunger.)
- Envision a purpose for your writing beyond "getting the assignment done."
  - A personal connection to your writing makes you more invested in what you are writing, and writers tend to write more effectively when they are interested in their subject.
  - Having a purpose also helps you to make decisions about what to include and what to leave out of your essay.

My aim is to put down on paper what I see and what I feel in the best and simplest way.
—Ernest Hemingway

Visual Rhetoric in the Composition Classroom

Allison Cooper

You probably know by now that rhetoric is deliberate and effective communication, but did you know that communication doesn't always have to be verbal or written? In your first semester of English, you probably didn't expect to engage in a discussion about art, advertisements, or movies, but these things have much in common with writing—namely, they can all try to persuade you through argument techniques. The same principles that apply when you analyze a speech or paper for rhetoric can also be used to analyze images. You can ask: What kind of *logos* does the image use? Do the images create an *ethos?* How does an image use *pathos* to appeal to you? Here are some tips on how to identify visual rhetoric.

Images, just like essays or speeches, often try to persuade using facts and authorities. When analyzing for *logos:*

- You might look for use of statistics. Does the commercial tell you that 9 out of 10 dentists prefer a type of toothpaste? If so, it is trying to persuade you based on *logos* support.
- You might look at the way images are placed beside each other. The sequence of images in a commercial or movie ask you to draw comparisons between two or more ideas, and in this way they try to "lead" you to the correct interpretation.
- Does the ad or commercial use a celebrity? If so, they are trying to persuade you with logos based on an "authority," in this case, a celebrity endorsement. Ask yourself, what does that celebrity *really* know about the product he/she endorses?

Images also establish an *ethos*—a certain type of credibility—so that you will be persuaded to "trust" their content. When analyzing for *ethos:*

- You can look for compositional elements like type (font) placement, types of images used, and general layout. If the images are clean, with regular lines and predictable patterns, the ad may be trying to appear

trustworthy in order to persuade you. If the images are jagged, wild, or unpredictable, the ad may be attempting to persuade you through spontaneity.
- ❏ Think about the company logo. Is it mild, conservative, and responsible? Or does it seem rebellious or cutting edge? Like the use of layout and fonts, the logo usually reflects the "personality" of the product.
- ❏ Consider the tone of movies and commercials. Is there a narrator who sounds firm, serious, and reliable, or does the narrator sound upbeat and fun? Narration and music can be cues to what type of ethos is being established.

Pathos is the easiest type of visual rhetoric to identify, because you can use your own emotions as an indicator. When analyzing for *pathos:*

- ❏ In print images, think about the emotional responses you have when viewing them. Is the image of someone crying or laughing? Is the image of a child? Is it a war scene or is it a holiday scene? The choice of images used cues you on how you should respond emotionally.
- ❏ In movies or commercials, consider what type of music is played. When you finish viewing it, how do you feel? Do you feel energized, tearful, or even hungry? If you have an emotional reaction, it might be because of the music or because of a narrator's voice, directing you to respond to the images presented.
- ❏ Do the images tell a story? Much like writing a narrative essay, images can remind you of history, ask you to question the present, and project ideas for your future. When you look at print or motion images, try to analyze what story is being presented, and ask yourself why the story is told and what effect it is supposed to have on you as a viewer.

Most visual rhetoric relies on a combination of *logos, ethos,* and *pathos,* and, because images are instantaneous, they often can be even more persuasive than the written word. The best way to approach visual rhetoric is to begin thinking critically about what you see. Remember that images are often chosen deliberately to persuade you, so whether you're viewing a painting or a movie, ask yourself what type of argument the images make. Once you are aware of the persuasive potential of images, you can then decide for yourself whether or not to believe what they "say."

Theory into Practice: Visual Rhetoric

While watching the movie Big Fish *Daniel found several connections between the screen images and his life. The pathos of the movie made him reflect on his own history, views and future. In this excerpt, watch how Daniel applies the visual narrative on the screen and the images and ideas they project to his own life. Daniel's paper is an example of how rhetoric, whether written or visual, is used in our daily activities, from watching a movie on a Saturday afternoon to writing a paper after midnight. Rhetoric influences us all.*

"Big Fishes: A Testimony to Life"

Daniel Stine

The greatest testimony to the richness of an individual's life is best demonstrated by those who show up at their funeral. In the film *Big Fish*, Edward Bloom's adventure that he calls life comes to an end. A large, diverse number of honest and true friends, whose lives were touched by Edward somewhere along his journey, were brought together one afternoon at his funeral to pay their respects. I would like to think that my funeral will have a familiar setting when my adventure, that I call life, finally comes to an end. They come because they know that they have been loved and accepted for who they really are.

Adaptability is a significant trait that Edward and I share—the ability to adjust and search for ways to fit in and thrive in our surroundings without compromising who we are. We have the potential to become "big fish" wherever we go. When Edward left his hometown for the first time, a place where he was well-liked and popular, he soon realized that he was not in a little pond any more. It was an ocean out there, but that didn't stop him from pursuing his dreams and getting what he wanted out of life. His drive and optimistic approach to life pushed him forward and earned him the respect of others. Growing up in a military family, I have lived in Germany, Kentucky, Louisiana, and several locations in Virginia and Hawaii. Sometimes I would stay in place for a year, sometimes two years, but never more than three. In each place, I have been able to start a fresh life, but I always have a goal that is similar to Edward Bloom's—to hang on to my ambitions and to learn from and respect those around me who also have dreams of their own.

In a scene in *Big Fish,* Edward bravely confronts the feared giant of the town and an unlikely friendship is born. He does not view the giant as the rest of the town does. Along the way, he meets other similar characters. He recognizes and respects the inner person of the giant, the witch, and everyone else who comes across him on his quests in life. The giant's deformity represents the character flaws that each and every one of us has. Unfortunately, I have found that many people do not take the time or choose not to look past human flaws, whether they are physical, mental or emotional. Edward, like myself, accepts the inner person above all else. I look around me as a freshman at college in yet another new surrounding, and I meet people who remind me of Adam—the neighbor down the street when I was in middle school, who at only twelve years old had been labeled an outcast. He had emotional and physical scars from a car accident and other problems within his family. I compare the scene where Edward is outside the cave where the giant lives (or was banished) to the time that I went to Adam's house and saw him sitting in his basement by himself at dinner time eating a sandwich and looking very lonely. I remember, I understand, and I look at the character of Edward and appreciate his genuine acceptance of others.

Revision: Take Two, Take Three...

Liz Vogel

The best writing is rewriting.

–E.B. W<small>HITE</small>

Revision might not be what you think. It's not about putting a comma here or changing one itty bitty word. Revision is a way to re-think, re-see, and re-conceptualize what you wrote. Revision is your friend. It offers you a second chance. When in your college assignments do you get a second chance? Well, in English 101, you do when you revise. Sometimes you even get a third or fifth or sixth chance. In fact, your success in the course is absolutely dependent on revision.

Let me try to explain what revision is about. Let's say you have a thought or idea or feeling about one of your writing assignments, so you write this down. Well, these words might be exactly what you wanted to say, but maybe they're not. Maybe you don't even know what you wanted to say. (I never do.) But, after you read what you've written, you realize that you had a whole lot more to write or your idea needed to go in a more interesting, exciting direction. Here's your opportunity to revise.

Revision (when you are thinking about what you wrote and making changes to your words) allows you to follow your writing where it leads you. People call first drafts "rough" for a reason. Words that go from brain to paper are often far, far from what you really wanted to write or what you have the potential of writing. Experienced writers know this. Hemingway supposedly wrote nineteen drafts of the final chapter to *A Farewell to Arms*.

Keep in mind that revision is a completely individual process for each writer and there is no one right way to do it. Some writers must revise line by line. Some write a whole draft, put it aside, re-read, make changes and then put it aside again. Revision can and should be done for the whole draft and then on smaller parts, like paragraphs or sentences. The truth is that one leads to the other. If you revise one sentence, you might decide that the whole draft needs to change. You might make a change and then decide later on that you liked your original phrasing better. That is fine, too. The point is to see revision as a process, both reflective and constructive.

Those first words that you put on the page are just the beginning steps to your writing assignment and those first words are rarely going to be your best words. First drafts are for exploration. They help you discover your ideas, but might not be fully developed. With each subsequent draft, you can organize your thinking, and thus, your writing. You can cut out ideas that do not go along with your overall meaning, and connect the ideas that remain. You can decide if a detail is specific or too general. On a second, third, or fourth draft, you might want to think more about your audience. Imagine, for example, someone reading your work. Have you communicated what you meant to say? Of course, any decent revising process includes taking care of grammar and spelling as a necessary but final step. Remember, fixing the semicolons and spelling might make your paper seem neater, but that isn't the kind of revision we are talking about. No one wants to read a perfectly punctuated paper that has no focus or is too general.

Ultimately, revision helps you get your ideas, feelings, or thoughts translated onto the page. Revision is a way to put forth your best writing, your most original thoughts. Re-reading your work and re-writing, thus "revising" your writing allows you to dig deep, to stew on an idea, to bring forth every ounce of originality and intelligence that you have within you. This idea guides our composition program, as well as our teaching and evaluating practices. Your instructor most likely will give you class time to revise, either with a workshop group or on your own. Your final grade will almost certainly reflect the amount of thoughtful revision you have done. Simply put, revising in English 101 gives you the chance to do your best work and illustrate your progress through your assignments and portfolio.

Vladimir Nabokov wrote, "I have rewritten—often several times—every word I have ever published. My pencils outlast their erasers." Nabokov knew the importance of revising. You should, too. Your knowledge of revision will free your first drafts because they won't have to be perfect the first time. Your use of revision will teach you that in writing, it's never too late for a second chance (or third or nineteenth).

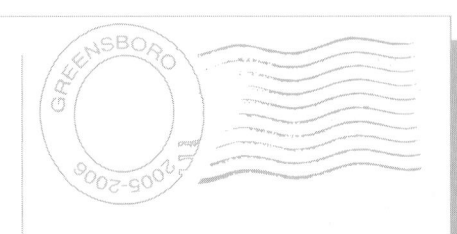

All You Ever Wanted to Know about 101
(But Were Too Afraid to Ask)

Reading Actively

Laura Savu

Each text contains its own interpretation, or dream. As readers, we tease the interpretation out of the dream, but while doing so, we are dreaming too.
—Kenneth Burke

All of my books end on an ambiguous note because nothing ever is that neatly tied up; there is always another beginning, there is always the blank page after the one that has writing on it. And that is the page I want to leave to the reader.
—Jeanette Winterson

In the case of good books, the point is not to see how many of them you can get through, but rather how many can get through you—how many you can make your own. A few friends are better than a thousand acquaintances.
—Mortimer Adler

English 101 challenges you to look at both writing and reading as creative, interpretive processes, driven by intuition as well as deliberate strategies. Together with your personal experience, reading will provide not only the context but also the pretext for the writing you will be doing in this class. Indeed, you will find that many of the reading assignments are keyed to your writing projects, requiring that you read from the perspective of rhetoricians, creative writers, fieldworkers, or scholars. This is because reading and writing are closely interrelated: What you know as readers can help you produce more effective writing; by the same token, what you learn as writers can help you accomplish more engaged and analytical readings—of your own and others' texts.

Besides reading for writing, some other reasons for reading may include reading for information and insight, for models of effective writing, for strengthening your language skills, and, of course, reading for fun. No matter how daunting the reading task seems to you, think of it as an opportunity to grow in knowledge, understanding, and imagination. Reading can enrich your life, as you become conscious of values, opinions, and cultures that are different from your own.

Since real intellectual exchange—what college education is all about—begins only when you react to what you read, you will be encouraged to analyze, defend, or question ideas you encounter in your readings, and to make connections among these ideas and your own experience. Most English 101 instructors will require that you keep some kind of reading journal in which, by recording your responses, impressions, and feelings about a reading, you're creating a parallel text of your own. As active, critical readers, you will be expected not to merely reproduce the words or thoughts of others, but rather reflect on them and then express your own thoughts. When doing so, you may find that sometimes you read things into texts that are simply not there. Not to worry: after all, the same text holds different meanings for different readers. At worst, your interpretation may indeed be flawed; at best, it will show that you have been inquisitive, skeptical, open-minded, and sensitive to both content (what is presented) and form (how ideas are presented). Like writing, reading with a critical eye is a skill that takes time, practice and yes, a certain discipline to acquire. For it is rather hard to make analytical points about a text you have read only once, and then when you were tired, distracted, or pressed for time.

To help you get the most of your readings, we would like to recommend some strategies that might prove useful in all of your classes:

1. Find or create the reading environment that feels most comfortable to you.
2. Prepare by considering the purpose for the reading. Why has the teacher assigned this reading? Where does this reading fit in the course syllabus?
3. Prepare to become part of the writer's audience. Read the introductory notes or any bibliographical or biographical entries in order to learn as much as you can about the writer, the circumstances (time and place) in which the piece was written, the kind of work he/she wrote, the writer's anticipated audience.
4. Prepare by pre-reading:
    - Look at the title of the piece: Does it suggest what the reading will be about? Does it suggest the writer's approach or attitude as well?
    - Scan the subheadings (if any): what do they suggest about the structure of this piece?

- Are there graphics/illustrations accompanying the text? How are they effective or useful?
- Look at the index to see if topics you are interested in are included.
5. Read the opening and concluding paragraphs to get a sense of the main ideas that are usually summarized in these sections.
6. Ask questions: What do I already know about this subject? What do I expect to learn about it from reading this piece? What is the author's purpose in writing this work? Is it to instruct, to inform, to entertain, to argue a point, to analyze a topic, etc.?
7. Read actively: Skim the reading to get a first impression of how the piece is written.
    - Do a second reading, slower and more reflective than the first. Break long texts into manageable units. During this stage:
        - Annotate the text: make marginal comments, jot down questions, underline/highlight key passages; put question marks by ideas/details you find confusing; circle unfamiliar words, figurative language, etc. Use a dictionary and/or encyclopedia to look up words, places, names, etc.
        - Consider the tone of the piece, the relationships among the ideas presented, the pattern of development. Is the author comparing and contrasting, moving from general to specific, showing cause and effect, or exploring a problem and solution?
    - Review your reading and annotations. Go back over particularly illustrative examples, reread confusing or intriguing sections, look for a key phrase that will clarify an idea. Pay attention to the nuances, subtleties, and implications of certain passages.
    - Reflect and evaluate, connecting the reading with other parts of the course and other parts of your life. What do other writers have to say on the same topic? What in your life is similar to this author's experiences or ideas?

Other points to remember:

- Comprehension and analysis *precede* evaluation.
- If you get stuck in the reading, record and explore your uncertainty and confusion. Consider the source of your reader's block and how you might overcome it.
- The above reading strategies will also help you gain the distance necessary for examining and critiquing your own work during the revision process.

- Sharing your thoughts about your readings in class and group discussions can open up new lines of thinking and thus produce more ideas for writing.
- What you read becomes part of your experience for later use.

Theory into Practice: Reading Actively

The following excerpts from Michael's essay, "Japanese Internment," delve into the issues found in Otsuka's book When the Emperor was Divine. *By actively reading the book, Michael is not only able to pinpoint the uniqueness of Otsuka's book, but also he can differentiate between the book and the official documents about the same event. In addition, Michael evaluates the relationship between the Japanese Internment camps and his own evaluation of U.S. history.*

"Japanese Internment"

Michael Rawls

Japanese Internment was one event in history that was kept out of the curriculum in schools, as a result many people don't know about it. What little people do know about it comes from the extremely ethnocentric views of the United States. This is saying that the United States is the superior nation and it was in our best interest to place the Japanese in the internment camps. We learn from articles such as Roosevelt's *Executive Order 9066* and DeWitt's *Instructions to All Persons of Japanese Ancestry* that it was necessary to put the Japanese in the Internment Camps. The United States felt that after Pearl Harbor was bombed the Japanese in America were a threat to society. However, history rewrites itself everyday with new findings and books such as *When the Emperor was Divine*, by Otsuka. What a book gives you as opposed to Official Documents is the use of emotion. Books appeal to the reader's emotions whereas Official Document are straightforward and don't have emotions in them. Instead of only having official documents we now have books that describe and show how terrible the Japanese people were treated. This is problematic because Otsuka uses emotion to persuade her audience to accept her feelings and beliefs about the internment. Her beliefs are that the internment process was wrong. Before books like this, people only thought about how the U.S. was right in doing what they did, but when you have both sides to argue you can form your own opinion. The U.S. government doesn't want their citizens to believe that they did something wrong but now they will have proof, Otsuka's book, which was based on her family's experiences in the internment camps. This book rewrites history because we now have new opinions and can empathize with the Japanese about the situation, which we couldn't have done before. The reason we can empathize with the Japanese is through the author's use of emotion to persuade the audience and cold hard facts that official documents just don't offer the public. Nobody wants to be taken from their homes and put into concentration camps in the middle of the desert away from civilization, for no reason whatsoever.

. . .

One thing that is not mentioned in the Official Document is how bad the conditions in the camps were. In Dewitt's and Flower's documents, there is not even a mention of the camps. The main reason for this is because the government doesn't want the citizens to think that the internment was bad and the camps were horrible. Some would dare to say that they resemble the concentration camps Hitler used on the Jews. However, the novel *When the Emperor was Divine* is centered on the life, or lack thereof, of a family in the camps. The desert in which the camp was located in ". . . was not like any desert he had read about in the books . . . no palm trees, no oases . . . there was only the wind and the dust and the hot burning sand. It was ninety-five degrees out. One hundred. One hundred and ten" (Otsuka, 53). One of the hardest parts about living in the camp was the dust. "He would always remember the dust. It made your nose bleed . . . your eyes sting . . . it took your voice away . . . the dust got into your shoes . . . your hair . . . your pants . . . your mouth . . . your bed" (Otsuka, 64). Who could live in a place like this? No one can be comfortable in one-hundred-degree weather, especially when you have no air-conditioner or a fan. The dust the little boy alludes to describes just how horrific it was. If your have ever had a stinging feeling in your eyes you know how bad it hurts. They continuously had these feelings due to the dust. These people couldn't even get a good night's sleep because the dust would come "under the doors and around the edges of windows and through the cracks in the walls" (Otsuka, 64). The dust acted as a plague upon the Japanese people because it was always hindering them from having a good day. It would burn your eyes, get into your clothes, make your nose bleed, and dry out your throat. The United States is very symbolic of the plague. We hindered the Japanese by completely cutting them off from society and putting them in internment camps. Why wasn't any of this put in official documents such as Dewitt's or Flower's? Were we not the bad people in this era? We were wrong for putting these people in the camps and I don't think that the United States wanted to admit that they were wrong for doing what they did. That's why you never hear the internment process mentioned in History class.

. . .

One thing that a novel gives the reader that a historical investigation cannot is the emotional standpoint of how someone feels. One night the boy ". . . woke up crying . . . Sometimes he worried was he there because he'd done something horribly wrong. But then he tried to remember what that horrible, terrible thing might be, it would not come to him" (Otsuka, 57). He thinks everything that's going on is his fault. When in actuality, it is the American's fault. How can you be so scared of an innocent little child? The little boy doesn't know what is going on because he is too young to understand. All he knows is that he is in a horrible place for some reason. He thinks it is because of him yet he had nothing to do with it. This part appeals to my emotions because the boy is crying and blaming himself because he thinks it is his fault for being made to stay here. He is being punished for someone else's wrongdoing yet he doesn't even know that. This appeals to the reader's emotions because we all know that the little boy had nothing to do with him being put in the camps. He is now blaming himself for everything that is going on and you have to feel sorry for him. This little innocent kid is blaming himself for something that should have never happened. It's the ignorant American's fault because the government forced the Japanese to be put in the camps.

We rewrite history everyday by finding out new things by archeologists digging up artifacts and recording data that changes our history. However this novel, even though it is fiction, rewrites history dramatically. Before I read this book, I thought that the internment was a bad thing, but I didn't know the half of it. The camps tormented these people. The people were U.S. citizens being detained for no reason. A whole race singled out for something that another country did. They were evicted and detained only because they were of Japanese Ancestry. The only good thing that came out of the internment was the fact that the U.S. acknowledged that the internment was a terrible injustice and they had been given formal apologies by the U.S. government.

Why Are the Readings Such a Pain? A Case for Complexity and Critical Theory

Sara Littlejohn

You have a reading assignment due before class tomorrow. You start reading the essay and quickly realize that it's going to take three times longer than you thought it would. To make matters worse, nearly every sentence requires a dictionary. Usually at this moment, you may be asking the question, "Why on earth does my professor want me to read this? This essay doesn't make any sense!" Don't worry. It's not supposed to make sense, at least not right away. If you were already supposed to know and understand everything we ask you to read, there really wouldn't be any reason to go to college, would there? Your English teachers want you to read, think, and come to class prepared to sort out what makes sense *and* what doesn't.

As students, part of the pressure to clearly understand everything you read comes from the belief that most of what you do in school should make complete and total sense. We certainly hope that assignments will be orderly and understandable, but as you go through college, you start to realize that ideas aren't always that simple. In fact, many concepts are quite complex, and the reading assignments often deal with this complexity. Many times, in order to communicate different, challenging or unique ideas, writers must use language that is equally as different and challenging, and at times your teachers will select assignments that ask you to engage with that complexity.

One of the most important ways that you can engage with that complexity and develop your analytical skills is to read with a different viewpoint or "lens" than you are accustomed to. Imagine if you heard the story of Cinderella from the point of view of the mice. Their view of events would be understandably different. In English studies we refer to these "lenses" as critical theory. Critical theory gives us the language to look at and talk about texts in different ways. Gender Theory, for example, suggests that when we read we can look at the ways that male and female characters and relationships are portrayed in a text. Are they stereotyped? Are the men and women valued equally by the writer, by society? Are men or women silenced in some way? Are they empowered? If you look at Cinderella through the lens of Gender Theory, you might ask why Cinderella waits for the handsome prince to save her. Why doesn't she save herself? And what message does this send to boys and girls who see this story everyday? Critical theory questions like these start to touch on issues that all of us face—right now, everyday—about what people expect from each other and why they might have those expectations.

The language and viewpoints of critical theory can give us greater insight into a work, so don't let the complicated language bother you. In the end, you will find that complexity and critical theory can deepen our understanding of texts and ultimately the world around us.

Here are some suggestions to help you weed through dense readings:

- If the essay is on Ereserve or Blackboard, print it out. It will be easier to read.
- Remember the rhetorical triangle: What claim is the author making? What is the author trying to persuade you to believe? Also, see the article "Rhetoric! Huh. What Is It Good For?"
- This claim is usually on the first or second page. Once you find it, underline it to help you remember it as you read.
- As you read through the essay, stop at the end of every paragraph and see if you can summarize in a sentence or two what the author is saying. Does it support the author's claim?
- If you read words you are not familiar with, underline them and look them up. This seems like a hassle, but in the long run, it can make the difference between understanding the reading and not understanding it. This serves two purposes.
- The underlining helps you remember the word in the future.
- Once you look it up, write a quick synonym or definition in the margin, so you can reference it easily.
- Once you have made it through the entire essay, ask yourself, did the author prove his/her claim?
- And remember not to get frustrated. Anytime we are exposed to something new, it takes some time to absorb it.

So Happy Together: Making the Most of Group Assignments

Robert Brandon

It is inevitable. At some point, one of your instructors will ask your class to work in groups, and despite the mixed emotions that many of us have towards group work, it is an important educational tool. Research has shown that cooperative and collaborative learning offers us the opportunity to develop communication and higher level thinking skills. It also allows us to interact with and share our ideas with our peers. Unfortunately, many of us feel uneasy in group situations or have had poor experiences working cooperatively in the past. However, by following several easy steps, you will be able to make your group assignments much more satisfying and useful.

One of the most important things that you can do to create a positive group atmosphere is to assign roles to each member. We have all been in groups in which nothing got accomplished because everyone was doing their own thing, or worse, in which one person did all the work while everyone else watched. Assigning each group member a role prevents such problems and gives everyone a sense of ownership of the assignment. You might find some of the following roles useful and your instructor might assign some others as well:

- Chairperson: Every group needs someone to coordinate the activities and lead the discussions. A chairperson shouldn't dominate the group or do all the work. Instead, they should strive to make sure that everyone is on the same page and that work is progressing at a steady pace.
- Recorder: Many assignments require that the group create a written document of their progress, and fulfilling this requirement is the recorder's job. A recorder might also take notes on group discussions and decisions in order to expedite the process.
- Spokesperson: Your instructor will often ask that the group report on their findings or discussions. It is the spokesperson's job to take the group's work and present it to the rest of the class. Depending on the size of your group, you may want to have several spokespersons.

If you have a group that works together on more than one assignment, it is a good idea to rotate roles. This gives everyone an equal opportunity to participate and allows people to see things from new perspectives. It is also essential to note that if you aren't assigned a role for a particular session you are not resolved from responsibility. It is everyone's job to provide the ideas and solutions to the assignment. Be active and be involved.

Once the task is underway, it is important to show your respect to everyone in your group. It is very easy for one or two vocal people to control the discussion, but everyone must be allowed to speak. Sometimes it is helpful to ask less vocal members direct questions so that they feel comfortable responding. Remember, it is a good practice to try to use at least one idea from each member of the group, so make this a goal for your group. Find something nice to say, even if it's a stretch. Even the worst of ideas has something to offer, if you just look hard enough. Focus on the good, praise it, and then raise any objections or concerns you have about the rest of it.

Eventually, even the most cohesive group will run into disagreements. When discussing difficult or controversial ideas, the group will be much more successful if everyone is taken seriously and allowed an equal voice. Thus, it is important to let everyone talk even if you disagree strongly with what they are saying. When such disagreements arise, it is the perfect opportunity to put your problem-solving skills to work. Using cooperative problem solving rather than coercive, intimidating, or non-inclusive methods to resolve conflicts and make decisions that benefit groups in multiple ways. Consider using some of the following steps to solve particularly tough problems:

- ❏ Understand All Points of View: It is important to allow individuals to share the reasoning behind their positions, which focuses problem solving on how to address underlying needs and interests and facilitates finding effective solutions. Make sure that you listen carefully to what everyone is trying to say before condemning anyone's idea.
- ❏ Brainstorming Solutions: Once everyone's position is understood, the group should brainstorm possible compromises that will allow the group to solve the problem. Again, it is easy to be dismissive of ideas that you disagree with, but it is often more useful to find common ground between two positions.
- ❏ Evaluating Options: Once a list of options has been generated, group members assess each option to identify which ones seem most promising to the assignment at hand.

- Agreeing on a Course of Action: Ultimately, the group should decide on the best course of action together and should make sure that everyone is clear on how the idea will be used in the assignment.

Hopefully, these ideas will help you make your groups more cohesive and more successful. Remember, the ultimate goal of working in groups is to pool our ideas in order to create more meaningful work and to allow us to experience the diversity that our university offers. Take advantage of it.

> *Every artist joins a conversation that's been going on for generations, even millennia, before he or she joins the scene.*
> —JOHN BARTH

Workin' It: Workshops in the Classroom

David Rogers

DOH! It is 8:30 in the morning, your English 101 class meets at 9:00 am, and you are in the computer lab printing out copies of a draft of your essay for English 101. In your mind, you wonder, "Is it good enough? Does it make any sense? Does it fit the assignment? Did I get my point across?" A sigh of relief enters your mind as you remember it is workshop day in your class, so you will have a chance to run your paper by your group before submitting a copy to your instructor. The writing workshop (also affectionately called "peer editing" or "peer workshop") provides you with a great opportunity to have a second, or third, or sometimes fourth set of eyes look over your work to help to tease out some of the same issues other writers wrestle with in their own writing. In fact, the writing workshop is one of the most important facets of any composition class, for it underscores the importance of revision, collaboration, and communication in the writing process.

You might be wondering: why do we have to workshop our papers at all? You are probably thinking: how are my peers going to know what the instructor is looking for in this assignment? Honestly, we have all grappled with these same questions. However, your peers are equipped to provide thoughtful suggestions to all of your work because they are dealing with the same issues, and it is often easier to recognize areas that need improvement in other people's writing than when it is your own. Our program believes that real learning takes place between the exchange of ideas through dialogue, and ultimately, this intellectual exchange helps us recognize how our own work matters in a larger context outside of the composition classroom. The writing workshop then gives students the opportunity to get feedback on their drafts and gives them a forum for bouncing ideas off one another. How can you strengthen your introduction? Does your conclusion ask new questions or does it simply summarize your argument? Do you successfully contextualize the passages you use to analyze? Is there a point in your paper where you are no longer staying on topic and focused)? Your peers can help you answer all of these questions. Additionally, when you are engaged in an intellectual dialogue with your peers and your writing, you might obtain new ideas that you have never thought of before. Think of the writing workshop then as a microcosm of the composition classroom. It's a space where you and your peers are the authority about writing and critical thinking, and you are there to ensure that everyone succeeds.

Below are a few suggestions to help facilitate a smooth workshop. Of course, there are many approaches to a successful draft workshop, but these should help you get started.

SUGGESTIONS FOR THE WRITER

1. Don't Be Lazy: Even if your instructor doesn't see a copy of this draft, being ill-prepared defeats the purpose of the workshop process. In other words, make sure you have a comprehensible draft before showing up to class. Not only is it disrespectful to yourself, but it is also disrespectful to your peers. Remember that writing is a process, so it's okay if you don't have a completely finished essay or if there are holes and flaws.
2. Ask Good Questions: A successful workshop depends on your eagerness to seek help. Don't ask your readers questions like, "Does my paper flow?" Good questions might include, "Is my thesis statement legible?" and "Do I need more textual evidence to support my position?" and even "Are there moments in my paper where you don't follow my argument?"
3. Talk To Me: Your readers have read your paper and provided their feedback. What next? Read over their comments and questions. Ask them more questions. If you don't understand a comment or question, ask for clarification. This exchange sharpens not only your own revision skills but also your readers'. Lastly, if you don't agree with their suggestions, explain why you made the choices you did and ask them to talk more about theirs. And remember to thank your reader.
4. Are You Talking To Me?: Don't get offended. We are all very close to our own writing because we often envision the process as an extension of ourselves. Be open to hearing their advice and criticism, and don't take it as a personal attack. This is your essay, so you don't have to take every suggestion your peers make, so be selective and thoughtful. However, remember that your peers are only trying to be helpful.

SUGGESTIONS FOR THE READER

1. Hold Your Horses: Take your time reading and responding to your peers' papers. There's no need to rush. Remember, you are here to help each other, so treat each paper as you would want your paper treated.

2. Comments Are the Spice of Life: Aside from the actual writing process, comments are perhaps the most difficult to articulate. There's nothing more frustrating than reading a comment that says "A Good Read." No matter how good you think your classmate's paper is, there is always something to say. Be as precise, concrete, and specific as possible. Don't you hate it when your instructor writes, "Confusing"?
3. The Grammar Police: While grammar and mechanics are important, at this stage in your peer's writing, you should be paying attention to larger problems rather than surface ones. Correcting a comma splice or a fragment is much easier than rearticulating a thesis statement or contextualizing a passage from the text. Feel free to point out grammatical errors, but do not limit your comments to these alone.
4. Be Courteous: Remember how sensitive you are about your own writing and give the same respect you would want to receive in return. We've all had a teacher from the past who made nasty comments on our papers. I was once told, "A donkey could have written this paper." Although this comment is HI-larious now, I didn't find the feedback helpful then and it wouldn't be helpful now. We are all adults, and the composition classroom must be a space for a free exchange of ideas. Constructive criticism is always the best approach.

The peer review can be one of the most rewarding experiences in your 101 classroom. The activity builds an intellectual community for writers to learn from one another.

The Portfolio: Watch It Develop

Todd Atchison

"Shake it like a pony white preacher." This was what I kept singing whenever I heard Outkast's "Hey Ya!" That is, until I consulted a lyric sheet. "Ohh," I said to myself, "it's 'shake it like a Polaroid picture'!" Things are much clearer now.

So why am I writing about "Hey Ya!"? Well, I think (to borrow from Anne Lamott) writing is a lot like a Polaroid picture; as you are going through the process, you never know what will develop. The act of writing is a sense of discovery; you'll find methods that work and drafts that won't; you'll learn to listen to that inner writing voice and to silence the critical ones; you'll let your imagination run wild with freewrites; and you'll encounter new ways of reading critically and writing well. What all of this amounts to is one word—*growth*. You will develop as a writer, as a reader, and as an intellectual student. This process will carry itself out through various writing assignments; these are snapshots of your progress. So, it is important to think of portfolios as a "family album" of all these Polaroid pictures from your semester.

Just as I misheard the lyrics to the song, you may have misinterpreted the purpose of portfolios. By the time you read this, you have more than likely had your first English 101 class meeting when you reviewed the syllabus. At one point during this dry reading of rules and regulations I'm sure that many of you shook like a pony white preacher after learning that there are only *two grades* for the semester: a mid-term and final portfolio. If this has you concerned, well, it should and it shouldn't. Let me explain.

Grades are little snapshots of your opinion on particular topics, entries of individual assessments that remove the coherent "big-picture" focus of your progress and abilities. While grades offer a more linear way of moving the class along, and they let you know where you stand at any given moment, this also offers thin data when summing up your abilities at the end of the term. This process also makes *you* more grades-driven than process-driven, and your focus shifts more towards the end product than on the development of skills. And yes, you should be concerned about portfolios because this makes up the majority of your grade; therefore, you should take precautions to revise your paper several times before you are ready to hand in your final drafts.

But the bottom line is progress. Portfolios allow you to reflect on your growth as a writer and *you should be compiling this material all along.* If you do this, if you stay on top of things, the portfolio assignment at the mid-term and end of the semester will not result in such a big "freak out." This is a compilation of your writings. Throughout the semester you will discover what works and what will not; you'll also begin to hear that inner voice telling you, "use more pathos" (if you don't understand now, trust me, you will). You'll also hear when words or sentences sound awkward and you'll get goose bumps when it all just "falls into place."

Most teachers of English 101 will ask you to keep everything you write: in-class freewrites, journals, notes, rough and final drafts of essays, etc. Others may ask that you pick and choose your material. Whatever the case, your portfolio should contain examples of the several different kinds of writing and various drafts of each assignment. Usually, you will be asked to write a reflective essay that introduces your portfolio. This gives you the opportunity to reflect on your strengths and weaknesses, the rhetorical approaches you've made within each piece, how your writings relate to readings in the course, and to consider your overall progress as a writer.

Pictures are all about focus (or lack thereof—it depends on your purpose). They're also about development. Think of writing each assignment as the shaking of that Polaroid. Pen to paper, or fingers on the keyboard, you realize you are going through a process. Learn to take the time to watch it develop.

English Composition Portfolio Contest

This past year the English Department had our first annual portfolio contest. This contest demonstrates our beliefs that writing is about more than individual assignments. We look at your writing experience in 101 from start to finish. The portfolio making process is an essential part of your 101 class. Through selecting and choosing your favorite writing pieces, you are able to reflect upon what you've learned about the writing process.

Several students submitted their work for our panel's consideration. We were so impressed by the hard work and effort put into your portfolios. This year we hope for an even wider participation. As you move through the semester, consider entering your own portfolio in our contest. Talk to your instructor if you would like more information and be on the lookout for guidelines for next year's contest.

LAST YEAR'S WINNERS INCLUDED:
First Place:
    Chikanele Adanna Emekauwa

Second Place:
    Cari Swann

Third Place:
    Lakashanna Corpening

Honorable Mention:
    Michael Rawls

All Freshman Read

Each year the UNCG English Department chooses a book for the "All Freshman Read." You and all the students in English 101 will read the same book. This activity offers you the experience of reading a common book and fosters literary discussions inside and outside of the classroom. You will be able to communicate with people not only in your classroom but also on campus, placing you in the middle of a literary community.

Besides reading the same book, you can also enjoy the same fun experiences. Each year a speaker, usually the author, comes to discuss the book chosen for the "All Freshman Read." This activity connects you to the speaker and to the work outside of the classroom. You will be given the opportunity to ask the speaker questions from you or from your class as a whole. Furthermore, you may be asked to go outside of your classroom and discuss your ideas with others. You may be asked to re-write a portion of the book, research controversial topics, or lead book discussions.

Our job is to find a voice for our own age.

–Nikki Giovanni

"Can Someone Please Help Me Find My Voice?": Speaking in the Composition Classroom

Michelle Johnson

"Um, well, humanism is . . . well, none of the articles and books I read gave an exact definition . . . um, uh, different schools of theorists all come up with their own uh, theory, but basically the definition is . . . well, uh, if one could give a basic definition, even though the chances are someone, somewhere would refute it . . ." As my face turned various shades of pink and red and sweat droplets began to form in my armpits and on my forehead, I continued rambling for another five minutes. "Um, uh, well, perhaps, I'm not sure." I don't know if I will ever forget that cold November evening in my rhetoric class.

Why is it that every time I open my mouth in an academic setting I feel that I sound like an incompetent fool? Yes, I said it—incompetent fool. Tragically, I feel like I cannot formulate a complete, coherent, thought-provoking idea within 2-5 minutes of being asked a question. For most of my academic career I have kept my mouth shut, many times to have another student or the instructor enter into the dialogue of our classroom with precisely what I was thinking. Perhaps I was always worried that I would say the wrong thing.

When I am forced to participate, and have time to prepare, I like to have my ideas written out clearly. Often this approach backfires just as much as raising my hand. For example, my most recent offering for my History of the English Language class went over like a lead balloon. While reading verbatim my ideas, which I printed up before class, I forgot the importance of inflection—"Wha, Wha, Wha Wha"—*Once again, Amy Fost will be playing the role of Charlie Brown's teacher this evening. I'm sure you are all surprised.*

39

A Test from the Emergency Speaking in Class Service (ESCS)

Circle the letter(s) that best describe(s) you:

A. Does the above scenario sound familiar?
B. Do you often say, "I hate speaking in class because everyone else is smarter than me"?
C. Do you have nightmares the day before a presentation?
D. Do you hate it when an instructor calls on you in class?
E. All of the above

The majority of the American public would circle "E." Speaking in front of a group is a common phobia from childhood to adulthood. Imagine, then, what first-year college students experience. Starting college is scary enough—roommate drama, boyfriend/girlfriend trouble, money problems—only to be intensified when the professor says, "You all will be required to speak in front of the class on a daily basis." Immediately your insides contort and a gigantic lump forms in your throat. The good news is 95% of your fellow classmates feel the same way. The bad news is the remaining 5% usually dominates classroom discussions, leaving everyone else (including the professor) bored and aggravated.

You may be wondering: "Why can't I go to class, take notes, sit quietly, and leave?" Here is the answer: A good college education requires more than being an obedient robot that regurgitates information. It involves dialogue and inquiry. Questioning, searching, responding, debating, and explaining are fundamental to gaining knowledge. Well, you may ask: "What does this have to do with my *writing* class?"

You will spend the majority of your time in English 101 *questioning, searching, responding, debating, and explaining.* Of course you will write, but more importantly, you will talk about what you are reading so you will have a better understanding of what *to write.* There is nothing worse than sitting down to write a paper with no ideas or a one-sided argument. Speaking in the composition class will not only help you generate ideas, but it will help you clarify what you think you know and become more confident expressing yourself.

Furthermore, a significant portion of your grade is based on your participation. So, although you do have to write, you do not have to be a "master writer" in order to get a good grade. Take advantage of the opportunity to increase your grade by speaking on a daily basis. Speaking in class will not only improve your participation grade, but it also improves your writing. See, writing is not just about grammar and thesis statements. You can have the most profound ideas, with "big words" and "perfect" grammar, but your writing voice may be stiff, choppy, disjointed, or empty. Writing is about clear expression of ideas, rhythm, connections, and emotions. Speaking reinforces all these characteristics of good writing.

Here is a good strategy for first-year college students to begin the speaking journey in the classroom:

- The day before class, jot down questions or ideas that you thought of during the reading. Plan to share at least one of your insights the next class session.
- Support or counter another student's statement. You can do this without being confrontational. Try beginning your statements with "I agree with . . . because . . ." or "I have another perspective on the subject . . ." Do not be alarmed. Someone will disagree with what you said. Just remember that the person is disagreeing with a statement or idea, not with who you are.

The most important thing to remember is that it takes time to become comfortable speaking in front of a group of people. But, the more you practice, the more confident you will be. Also, only you hear "Wha, Wha, Wha, Wha, Wha." Your classmates and instructor care about what you have to say, and because 95% of the class feels the same way as you about speaking in class, they are not judging you. So, forget about the days of high school when students huddled in the hall or in the lunch room to crack jokes about what you said in class. And, hopefully, if you happen to take another test from the **ESCS,** you will have to pencil in your response: *F. None of the Above.*

Words That Start with "S"

G. Warlock Vance

When I was first assigned a 102S section of English Composition, I assumed the "S" didn't mean much of anything—just some sort of departmental code to differentiate one section from another. Then I found out it stood for "Speaking Intensive" and I panicked. *Does that mean that only the students can speak and I'm only allowed to write on the board, or worse, does it mean that I have to talk all the time and I'm not allowed to write at all?*

Thankfully, neither of these situations were an accurate description. The Speaking Intensive part of any 102 section means that, in addition to more in-depth writing experiences, students will also be given many opportunities to speak in front of their peers in class, in both casual and formal venues. The university hopes students will improve both writing and speaking skills and to learn various forms of argument and the means to get their point across in a cogent manner.

But, while the university asks all instructors to follow these and other guidelines, there are actually no set *rules* as to how 102S courses must be taught. With my own 102S classes I have particular ideas as to the level at which my students should be writing. I feel too many instructors talk down to their students. I never do this. I never underestimate my students' abilities to surprise me—in fact, I encourage it by providing exercises that challenge students' perceptions and open their minds to new ways of looking at the world in which they must work and live.

The average student who enters my 102S class has usually already worked their way through the more general 101 course. It is my desire that they can continue to build upon their composition experiences, to move farther along with their writing skills while simultaneously learning the importance of being able to express themselves verbally.

Of course, speaking in public can be a very frightening experience for some, but I provide students with a variety of opportunities to stand up and speak their minds. Some of these instances are more casual than others, but each one works in conjunction with the one before it to build confidence and precision.

Students are asked to make formal presentations based on extensive research, but they are also encouraged to perform skits and/or tell jokes. I might ask a student to take over my job in front of the class, to lead discussion for a few minutes. This gives them the ability to see the classroom and its occupants from my point-of-view, to understand that I am not simply an authority figure attempting to dump information into their brains, that I too am a person, very much like themselves, someone trying to communicate my ideas in both oral and written forms.

In my opinion, the "S" in 102S not only stands for "Speaking Intensive," but also for "Sharing" and for "Self." By learning how to hone one's skills as a writer and speaker it is possible to learn not only how to share information, but to share one's own personal experiences—those things that make us who we are.

The continued practice of these methods provides us all with opportunities to learn about one another and of our world. Utilizing our knowledge, through more adept means of written and oral communication, provides us with most excellent skills to know each other personally and culturally, to grow closer together physically and spiritually, and to learn the myriad ways that we might share the wisdom of our peoples, and our understanding of ourselves as individuals.

Student-Teacher Conferencing

Karen C. Summers

Sometime during the semester, you will be asked to meet with your instructor for a conference. This is a time for the two of you to talk one-on-one about your writing and to address any concerns you may have. A class such as English 101 may be a new experience for you, because it emphasizes writing as a process; that is, after you create a first draft, your paper will undergo one or more revisions. Feedback from your classmates and instructor is very important to the success of your paper because it can help you to see ways that you can communicate your message more clearly. Conferences with your instructor provide time to ask questions, review drafts, and discuss revision plans.

There are several different purposes for conferences, and your instructor may schedule them for different reasons at different times. At the beginning of the semester the goal of a conference may be to get to know each other a little better and share information about your previous writing experiences. Once a paper has been assigned the student and instructor may meet to clarify the assignment, brainstorm for ideas, or create a plan of action. Later on in the semester you may meet to review drafts, discuss your progress, and find ways to overcome any difficulties you have encountered. Your instructor will inform you of the purpose of the conference and tell you what you should bring with you. And remember, you can schedule a conference with your instructor whenever you would like simply by making an appointment with him or her. When you were in high school, you may have thought of a conference with your teacher as something negative. A conference at this level is a completely different thing—it is a professional collaboration between the two people who care most about your writing.

As your conference time will probably be only between 15-30 minutes, it is important to be prepared so that you can make the most of the time. Make sure you know where your instructor's office, or the designated meeting place, is. Come with your draft, revision, or ideas for writing, whichever your instructor requests. Be on time! This is important because other students will be waiting for appointments, too, and if you are late you will push everyone else back. Think about what you want to get out of the conference. Many conferences focus on a draft of your writing assignment. Your instructor may have read and responded to a written draft before the conference takes place. You should expect to take an active role by reviewing what you have written and what feedback you have gotten so far, and deciding what you plan to do next. Bring paper and pen with you to take notes.

Often students wait for the instructor to "fix" their papers, but college writing does not happen in this way. These are your thoughts, ideas, and words; it is your responsibility to make the conference valuable by being prepared with ideas, or a draft, and with specific questions. You will decide what is most helpful to you to discuss. The instructor's role is to provide feedback and teach, not to take over your paper and make it his or her own.

When you leave the conference you should have some ideas that will help you revise. You should have devised a workable plan of action for your paper. As with any other skill, the only way to improve your writing is to practice. In time you will begin to be able to evaluate yourself—you will know your strengths and weaknesses, and what works in your writing. The goal of a conference is to help you learn these skills so that you become a more independent and effective writer.

Literature in the Writing Classroom

Lee Templeton

You may be surprised to discover that one of the many things you will do in English 101 is read and respond to pieces of literature. You may even ask yourself, "what does reading literature have to do with learning how to become a better writer?" The answer is very simple—everything. Reading and writing are so intricately linked that it is nearly impossible to talk about one without the other. In fact, the more you read, the more your writing will improve. Literature, whether in the form of fiction, poetry, drama, or essays, has a number of uses in the writing class—by reading and responding to literature you can practice your critical thinking skills, observe how various authors employ the very same writing skills you are learning, and become a more effective reader.

When you are asked to respond to a piece of literature, you are being asked to think critically about what you have read and express those thoughts in writing. The first place to begin is with your personal reactions to the text—how did you feel about the text? Did you like it? Hate it? Find it interesting or boring? Critical thinking begins when you explore *why* you reacted to the text the way you did. Maybe you were drawn in by the author's use of language, or the way she used description to set the scene and create a certain mood. Perhaps you found the author's tone to be out of place in the story he was telling. Or maybe you disagreed with the author's stance on certain social or political issues. The important thing to remember is that critical thinking requires you to move beyond a simple "I liked it" or "I hated it" response and examine what aspects of the text influenced your response.

When you begin to think critically about a text, you start to pay attention to how the author put the text together. In other words, you begin to notice how the author employed those writing skills that you will be using in your own papers. If you like the way a particular author opens a story, try to determine how she creates that affect and see if you can't use a similar approach in your own writing. Pay attention to the way these writers draw their audience into the stories they are telling, how they use specific details to create vivid scenes, how they weave their own reflections into the narrative, and how they manage to imbue their writing with a certain mood or tone. Let the literature you read in class inspire you to try new things in your own writing.

Finally, as you begin to think critically about the literature you are reading, and as you begin to pay attention to how the authors create their texts, you are becoming a stronger, more experienced, and more effective reader. This, in turn, will help you become a stronger, more experienced, and more effective writer. If you can identify what you respond to as a reader, what moves a writer makes that are the most effective, you can better anticipate what the readers of your essays will respond to. And as you will learn, being aware of your audience is an important part of writing well. Also, you will be a better reader of your classmates' work. English 101 involves a great deal of peer review and workshopping of papers, and the better reader you are, the more you can articulate what works well for you in an essay and what doesn't, the more helpful you will be to others in your class.

As you can see, reading and writing go hand in hand. Reading literature in your writing class is more than just a way to keep you busy—it is an integral part of the writing process.

The role of the writer is not to say what we can all say but what we are unable to say.

–Anais Nin

"You Want Me to Do What?": Assignments in the Composition Classroom

Journaling 101

Rita Jones-Hyde

In the composition classroom, writing takes on several guises, from a formal essay to a seemingly random free write. You might write a reflection of your reading experiences, a critique of a short essay, or an anecdote about your life. No matter what form your writing takes, the purpose is to expand your thinking skills and connect your thoughts to the page. In order for you to practice these critical maneuvers, most composition instructors require you to keep a collection of your thoughts in a journal, writer's notebook, or writer's log.

Each instructor has his or her individualized method of journaling. Some instructors schedule daily, weekly, or monthly entries, or they allow hand-written or typed journals. Your instructors might provide you with a writing prompt or topic while others let you choose a subject for each entry. Similarly, composition instructors vary their grading practices. Grading individual journals, including journals in portfolio grades, or disregarding grades and grammar entirely are all common routines. Always check the course syllabus for your professor's expectations. In any case, journals are a vital element of your writing experience. They offer you an opportunity to expand and express your thoughts in a somewhat stress-free environment. Journals help you recall original reactions to a short essay, class discussion, or assignment. A written account of your thoughts, experiences, and ideas produces paper topics for formal projects or instigates discussions in small groups. Outside of your 101 class, journals help you understand college experiences or reading assignments from various classes.

Regardless of how you arrange or use your journal, you should expect to spend time and effort on each entry. When you simply regurgitate information from class or wait until the last minute to write the entry, your journal is a burden rather than an asset. Most instructors require you to spend fifteen to thirty minutes outside of class for each entry. If you feel as though you simply do not have enough time for a journal, remember that your instructor is only asking for the same amount of time it takes to watch part of "The Simpsons" or the first half of "American Idol." Since journals require time and effort, do not discard your entries. Not only might they be required for your portfolio, but they also contain useful information for papers or mementos of your college experience.

Getting Started

Though the primary purpose of your journal is to strengthen your thinking and writing skills, journals also invite exploration into a variety of approaches to writing. Since most instructors take up journals several times during the semester, your journal could represent a conversation between you and your teacher. If your instructor uses entries for small group prompts, then consider your journal a dialogue in which you critique readings or share assignment ideas. Within the dialogue, you could summarize a reading assignment, express a concern, or ask a question. Go ahead and discuss a paper topic or test your knowledge of a reading assignment. Use the conversational characteristics of journals to your advantage.

Journals are also a place for you to record personal experiences; however, a word of warning: When writing about your life, remember that your journal is not a diary. You are not Bridget Jones, and this is not your movie. Instructors often appreciate entries that connect personal experiences with the class readings or discussions, but please only write stories that you feel comfortable sharing. Remember that your notebook does not have a lock or a key, and your teacher and perhaps even classmates will read your entries.

Commenting or reflecting on a particularly difficult or enjoyable text connects your journal with the assignment for that day and other readings throughout the semester. If you find that you did not have an opportunity to share your thoughts in class, then use your journal to finish the discussion. When taking this approach to your entry, it is helpful to compare and contrast works or to agree or disagree with classmates.

A final suggestion: unconventional writing explores the inner workings of your imagination and the entertaining art of composition. Try eliminating formal structures by telling a story from end to beginning or approaching a subject from a view that is not your own. Describe the local coffee shop from the perspective of a barista, or explain an essay from the author's point of view. Experimenting might also include writing your thoughts in the form of letters, screenplays, or poems. Since journal requirements vary from instructor to instructor, you should check with your teacher or make sure your imaginative approach meets the expectations of the course.

One Last Comment

When constructing your entries, remember to allow time to write and enjoy your journals. Take risks and explore the space and freedom created in the entries. Also, make journaling a vital element of your writing experience because good journaling practices could start your career as a writer or begin a long term written account of your life.

> *Writing is an exploration. You start from nothing and learn as you go.*
> —E.L. Doctorow

Writing the Reflective Essay
Laura Alexander

One of the most common assignments composition instructors give to their students is the reflective essay. While some instructors use this type of writing assignment as an initial project to assess students' individual writing processes, others assign the reflective essay to help students develop critical thinking skills—an important goal for any composition student. Still others see the reflective essay as a vehicle for overcoming barriers to writing.

For many writers, the reflective essay frees the mind from teacher-imposed prompts and can give writers a chance to create their own themes. Some composition students, however, find that it increases their anxiety because it *does* give more freedom. Unfortunately, this anxiety can lead to passive writing, or writing that reflects an emotional or even indifferent reaction rather than a critical response. And while it may seem like the reflective essay calls for your emotional response, such as "I hated that story" or "I loved that story," this is not the case. What the reflective essay actually asks students to do is think about how the writer constructs his or her language, ideas, and themes. For example, your instructor might ask you to write a reflective essay on Charlotte Perkins Gilman's "The Yellow Wallpaper." Your initial response might be "this is a crazy woman's obsession with tacky wallpaper." This response, an emotional one to the plot, can be turned into a critical response by reflecting on why you responded the way you did. Why do I think she's crazy? What made her that way? When does she seem crazy, and when does she seem sane? How is the wallpaper related to her sanity? When you begin to analyze your own reading of the text and ask questions about your reaction, you can begin to think critically not only about what you've read, but also about what you've written. The text and your thoughts interact because you reflect on them together, and this process leads to active rather than passive writing.

The first step to active writing is active reading—something the reflective essay necessitates. The successful composition student is one who thinks, reads, and writes actively and one who sees these activities as reciprocal. Take notes as you read, underlining difficult and interesting passages and looking up words you don't know in a dictionary. You can brainstorm alone or in a small group about ideas for potential essays or about texts you find difficult.

Remember that, although the reflective essay can take many forms, it asks you above all to think critically about your own ideas. If your instructor assigns a topic that involves your personal experience as a writer, then he or she wants you to think about the self in relation to the world and/or to a text. Think of the reflective essay as one that allows you to explore a topic I know you and your instructor want to understand better: you!

But have the courage to write whatever your dream is for yourself.
–MAY SARTON

Creative Writing in the Composition Classroom

Joe Wagner

This little essay is intended to do a couple of things: first, to let you know that many of your English teachers will probably ask you at some point during the semester to write "creatively," and second, to try to give you some idea of what that means. Most of you, I imagine, have been asked before to write "academic" papers in your English classes, papers that have a thesis, or main argument, support for that thesis with outside sources, an introduction and conclusion to help the reader along, etc. You'll probably still be asked to do this in some form or another in your writing courses here at UNCG, but you will also likely find an emphasis on, how shall I put it, "less academic prose" such as journal writing, personal narratives, and other writing that relies less on formal research and more on lived experience. I'll try to spell out a bit further here the distinctions, or more specifically the lack of distinctions, that many of us see between "creative" writing and "academic" writing.

It's my opinion that these two forms of writing have so much in common that to place them in separate categories is problematic. Some English teachers may disagree, but I would argue that both creative and academic writing have for the most part the same aims and that they both work to accomplish those aims in much the same way. For example, most of us would agree that academic writing needs a thesis, support for that thesis, coherence, voice, mechanics, and of course the catch-all that it's, you know, well written. These last four, coherence, voice, mechanics, and that well written thing, are certainly needed in creative writing as well. In place of a thesis, we might suggest here "theme," or "thread" that holds the story together. And in lieu of "support for a thesis," we might offer story development, character development, momentum, or "twines working towards a common thread," as it was once put. If it strikes you that the term "thread" is just a more creative way of saying thesis, and that "momentum" or "twines working towards a common thread" are just more creative ways of saying "support of a thesis," you're not alone. That's how a lot of us see it. In fact, I believe that teachers are looking for so many of these same things in both genres of writing that the line between an academic piece and a creative piece becomes hard to identify. Indeed, as Wendy Bishop suggests, "we need to be crossing the line between composition and creative writing far more often than we do. In fact, we may want to eliminate the line entirely" (46). Or, as Marie Ponsot and Rosemary Petrosky tell us, "student writing is literature . . . it is a product of imagination and thought. In our experience and the experience of those we know, there is no essential difference between writing a poem and writing an essay" (57).

Are Bishop, Ponsot, and Petrosky right? Are these two types of writing so similar as to be the same thing? Some may say no, but I think they are. Take, for instance, this little essay you're reading right now. Is it academic or creative? You could point to my citations of these three scholars as proof that it's an academic piece, or you could point to my use of the first person and my relatively informal tone that it's a creative piece. My point is not only that the labels "creative" and "academic" are often insufficient, but that you need not get overly anxious if you're asked to write something like a personal narrative related to the topics at hand; it's not really a different animal of writing than the more "academic" prose you might be used to.

What I've said here is meant to help in a rather general way—always, of course, follow the particular writing assignment you have in front of you, and ask your teacher if you have any questions about this issue. Again, don't be afraid to ask. That's part of our job.

Have fun.

Theory into Practice: Creative Writing

Apart from the research papers, personal narratives, and reflective essays in your composition classroom, you may be asked to write something different, something that makes you thoroughly use your imagination and creative powers. Ben, in the excerpt below, has creatively articulated his personal personae. Note how Ben's essay differs from the other writings you will be asked to do in class.

"A Buñuelian Experience"
Ben Barbour

A faint yet undeniable light, slicing through the night as if it were a butter knife making its way through a firm birthday cake, illuminates my face as I sit here on the back porch of my vacation home with my only companion, the August breeze. I find solace here from time to time, solace in sitting peacefully beneath the hanging stars; reassured that I could fall asleep amongst the full moon and chirping crickets, never once having to worry about what tomorrow brings. I wouldn't, after all, be disrupted by the maddening morning wake-up calls of screaming alarm clocks were I to nod off right here on the back porch in the comfort of my rocking chair. Oh yes, I can sleep in tomorrow. Hell, I can sleep on into Sunday if I wish.

But don't let that lead you to believe that I have no life, that I am some lazy sloth who does nothing more than rock-rock-rock the day away on my back porch. No, I have hobbies and I'll let it be known, right here and now, that I made my riches (yes, I am filthy rich) doing nothing more than what I enjoy. And what I enjoy is simply this, writing. In addition, it seems that many enjoy reading what I enjoy writing for I have thrice been published, thrice placed smack-dab upon the bestseller list.

Benjamin C. Barbour, as I have been called since the eventful day of my birth, is a name now synonymous with the murder-mystery genres of both literature and film; I have, in exercising my passion for the cinema, branched out as the director of the film adaptations of my novels (instantly hailed as a master). Benjamin C. Barbour is a multi-millionaire who, when on sabbatical between writing and film projects, seeks succor in the laid back atmosphere of his vacation home, a posh, beach-side mansion in Italy.

Interpreting Our World: An Introduction to Ethnography

Janet White

For those of you out there who cringe at the thought of writing yet another research paper, I have good news. I just saved a bunch of money at Geico. No, seriously, there really *is* good news. If you were hoping I was going to tell you that the current administration had placed a moratorium on research papers, I'm sad to say that you will be disappointed. The rest of you, however, will be delighted that I am going to share a little secret with you. It is a well kept secret that your high school English teachers vowed to keep from you as long as you walked their hallowed halls. You may want to sit down for this. Research doesn't have to be boring. Sick of consulting all of those painfully dull books and questionable websites only to find out what everyone else thinks? You don't have to. Instead all you need is a notepad, curiosity, and the ability to connect the dots. Think there's no "I" in research? Think again.

The process of ethnography involves studying people in the context of their lives. Rather than forcing us to rely on what the alleged "experts" say about a particular group of people, ethnography gives us the chance to become experts and see for ourselves. That opportunity eventually becomes a responsibility as we are asked to examine our own assumptions about the culture and reflect on our experiences in the field. That process of reflection means that *you* are the most important element in your ethnography. Without you and your own experiences and perspectives, your paper would be reduced to a meaningless pile of data. And let's face it. We don't need any more of that.

In the past, you have probably been told to leave yourself out of your research papers. You were probably told to collect everyone else's ideas about a given topic and present them in a coherent paper, leaving little room for your own voice. Ethnography is different. Not only are you *allowed* to insert yourself into ethnographic research, your presence is *required*. You are the lens through which we see your given subculture. Inevitably you are a part of your research. Understanding that fact is an important component of ethnography.

When preparing to write an ethnography, your instructor will ask you to select a subculture that you want to know more about. Then you will be asked to observe that subculture on several different occasions. During your observations, you will collect data in a variety of ways. You may conduct interviews with informants (the fancy name for members of your subculture). You may collect artifacts from your site. But most importantly, you'll take notes. To give yourself enough data to choose from, you'll need to write down everything. Pay attention to sights, smells, sounds. Just because you think something is insignificant at first doesn't mean it won't have greater importance when looking at the big picture.

When it is all said and done, your interpretation of the data is the most important part of the ethnographic process. Unfortunately, it is also the most difficult part. Lucky for you that you're already an expert at it. You interpret the world around you every day. Through conversation, body language, and people's dress, you probably draw conclusions about people on a regular basis. Doing ethnographic fieldwork enables you to expand that natural ability and make meaning on a larger scale. Instead of drawing conclusions about one person, you have the opportunity to use your evidence to create meaning of your entire experience in a subculture.

Ultimately, the ethnographic process will help you become better students and will even go a long way to enrich your membership in the larger community. The entire process will enhance your ability to draw conclusions while helping you realize the different types of evidence that support those conclusions. Furthermore, it will help you become more aware of the world around you and force you to challenge your preconceived notions about different groups.

Coming to terms with our attitudes about different groups can only help us recognize the inevitable connections we all share, which brings us back to that aforementioned desire to connect the dots. This is no paint by numbers; there is no prescribed outcome. You can take the same dots, draw different lines, and you'll have a different picture. You get to see the world in a whole new way. It's your world. What do you see?

Theory into Practice: Ethnography

In this excerpt, Ashley delves into her own attitudes and the attitudes of others about clubs in today's society. She has done research and visited on several occasions the sports bar in her essay. In addition, as the previous article discussed, throughout her essay, Ashley must come to terms with views of both hoppers and rabbits.

"The Club Hoppers & the Rabbits Outside"

Ashley Jones

The Sports Bar

As you walk through the "push-pull" glass doors you seem to walk into a place you never thought existed. The fresh smell of perfumed and cologned men and women fill the air. A smell so sweet it captures one's attention like the smell of home-made apple pie. As you look above you, the silver glitter thrown onto the navy blue ceiling seems to resemble the midnight sky on the clearest night in the month. The sixty or seventy circle tables, with their red legs and blue faces, surround you a few feet after walking in the door. The floor, like the ceiling, is splashed with silver glitter, which sinks into the grey backdrop. The music is so loud you might think you are in a music video, but you'll soon find out that none of the dances are made up by a choreographer. While taking all this in, you'll walk around, and come into contact with various objects and things to do. The six pool tables split into two rows on your left, the boxing ring with four loud speakers will consume the middle, and the four big screen TV's hanging above the boxing ring will also make you feel as if you are really at a sporting event; however, once you look to your right that thought will be dismissed. The DJ booth will be sitting there, with the wild colored lights hanging above his head, hitting the people on the dance floor in a wonderful contrast to one another. The two bars will allow you to see those who are over twenty-one, if you're at all interested, and the various sports memorabilia will remind you that this is no ordinary place. Of course the next thing you see will be the people that are here to let loose and dance the night away. All dancing to the same beat, yet looking so different, the people on the dance floor in front of the boxing ring will allow you to let go of all your problems of the day and have a good night.

The People

The females wearing revealing clothes play the part of the temptress, luring both single and involved men on the dance floor. The males maintain the cool stature, daring only the bravest females to make a move on them. No insecure partners will be tolerated tonight. Nevertheless, no one seems to be in a rush so there is no need to check the time or hurry to make sure you get your money's worth on the dance floor; the DJ will let you know when the club is closing. But that is the least of your concerns right now. The people are all so interesting, mostly due in part to the fact that everyone is so different. Attire, style, smell, physique, and dance techniques all set everyone apart from the people around them. Appearance is key in this type of environment.

Attire

The attire for the club is basically a "come as you are" type dress code. Sneakers, heels, boots, sandals; any shoe will do. The weather also has a lot to do with the way the "club hoppers" dress. Many young ladies had on jeans and some sort of t-shirt on this night. It was only thirty-five degrees outside, so to wear more than a skirt and a tank top was not optional, however, some females did opt for a skirt and sneakers. But as the days get warmer, I would assume, the clothing gets tighter and smaller. The males mostly sport some sort of t-shirt with a design or a button-up shirt with some khakis. Although there isn't much for the males to choose from, their personal style is what will get them noticed on this night. I noticed a particular guy who wore a t-shirt with a Hawks jersey, red and yellow fleece pants and a red and yellow fleece jacket. He accented this outfit with a Hawks hat, and even had on shoes that had red and yellow in them. He was one of the more. . ."well put together" gentlemen in the club. Some of the not so fancy men wore a simple one color t-shirt, jeans, and some sneakers. Either way, it seemed as if everyone was comfortable in what they had on, so I guess comfort is key in this club . . .

The End of the Evening

As we walked out of The Sports Bar into the chilly weather I saw a couple that danced separately leaving to go to their car. The seductively dressed young ladies now shivered with frozen limbs as they made their way to their friend's car to go home. As I walked to the car, cold and overjoyed with how much fun I had, I noticed something in the corner of my eye. With all the commotion around me, I managed to spot one of the quietest animals ever, a rabbit. He sat in the grass, hopping here and there, making sure not to get in anyone's way. In a way he reminded me of the people in the club; all moving to a rhythm yet managing to stay out of the way of the people around them.

Stage Fright— Minus the Stage

Tamara Wiandt

On my first day of teaching college English, I strode confidently into the classroom, smiled, faced the chalkboard . . . and proceeded to write my own name incorrectly. Yikes! Now panic set in. My palms began sweating, my heart began pounding, and I felt the butterflies in my stomach begin to do the mambo. The way I looked at it, I had two choices: I could pretend nothing was wrong and just keep going in this panicked state, or I could admit my own silly mistake and see what would happen. I chose the latter. I told my class that if they could manage to spell their names correctly, they would be doing better then me this semester already. We all got a good laugh out of it and the stage was set for a class where humor helped us overcome our nervousness.

So why is this story important? Well, besides giving you a good laugh at your instructor's expense, it lets you see that *everyone* gets nervous sometimes. What I would like to do now, is give you some practical tips for overcoming stage fright that I find helpful.

Pick-a-tic

Okay, this sounds a little weird, but by managing your nervousness by channeling it into one unnoticeable habit you can control it. For instance, whenever you feel stressed, squeeze your thumb and pointer finger together. Practice in line at the grocery store, while waiting for the librarian to find that book she swears is on the shelf, or while waiting for your roommate to get off the phone with her annoying boyfriend at two in the morning. After you've practiced this for a while, using this during class presentations or other speaking situations will be second nature. You will appear calm and relaxed and no one will ever know your secret.

Pre-presentation Relaxation

Duck into a restroom or other quiet place and try these quick stress release techniques.

Shake it up: For about ten seconds shake out all of your extremities from your hands to your feet and roll your neck and shoulders. By the way, don't worry if you feel silly since it's impossible to be nervous when you are laughing at yourself.

Reach for the sky: Pick a point on the ceiling, raise you hands over your head and reach for it ten times.

Collapse: Bend over at the waist and let your hands and arm hang loose. Roll your back up slowly until you are upright. Take a deep breath and walk to your classroom with confidence.

Other Suggestions:

1. Be totally prepared.
    a. Plan your presentation.
    b. Research and outline your topic.
    c. Cite your sources, if applicable.
2. Practice your talk several times out loud.
3. Take deep breaths before you're called to speak.
4. Don't hesitate to admit and discuss your apprehension with classmates and your instructor before the speech.
5. While waiting to be called, think only positive thoughts.
6. Realize that everyone in the audience is pulling for you, they want you to succeed just as much as they want to succeed when it's their turn.
7. Constantly remind yourself that there is no other person anywhere in the world like you and that your audience is looking forward to getting to know you.

Unfortunately there is no sure fire way to keep you from getting stage fright, but it might help to recall the old joke:

One night in New York a man asked a cabbie, "How do I get to the Met?" The cabbie replied, "Practice!"

That's the best advice I can give. Practice your material until you know it cold. Oh, and remember to breathe. Passing out cold in front of an audience is way more humiliating than anything you could ever say in a presentation.

A Rookie's Guide to Research

Temeka L. Carter

Ranked among the top fear-inducing college tasks, such as taking tests, quizzes, and presentations, is the research paper. Research writing is an aspect of academia that many students would choose to avoid if given the opportunity. Students are not generally enthusiastic about completing this time-consuming feat that breeds much uncertainty. However dreadful research writing may appear, feelings of trepidation can be overcome with a positive attitude and ample preparation. In addition, it can be rewarding to learn about a new subject and become something of an authority on it.

Since the structure and requirements for research writing may vary according to the teacher and course, make sure that you understand every aspect of your assignment. If you are confused and try to figure the assignment out on your own, you might waste many hours that would be best applied toward completing your paper. Being confused is intimidating and hinders you from producing your best work. If you have any questions about what your instructor expects—ASK! You can ask questions in class or meet privately with your teacher to ensure that you are progressing successfully.

Once you understand your assignment, it's time to start researching. Both the internet and Jackson library are good places to start. There is a research tutorial available at **http://library.uncg.edu/depts/ref/tutorial/** which will give you an overview of how to research a topic effectively. You can begin with the online library catalog and periodical indexes (using a computer in the library or at home) to find books, magazines, journals, and newspapers. Go to **http://library.uncg.edu/** where you have access to resources such as the library catalog, electronic databases, and journal finder. If you are unsure of how to proceed from here, use the tutorial or ask your instructor or a librarian. Many articles, and even books, are now available online; however, many are not, so it's always a safe bet to start in the library where you have access to printed copies of these materials. If you decide to use computer sources that are not related to the library, you can begin by using search engines such as www.google.com or www.yahoo.com.

After you have determined that your research will support your topic, there are three things to keep in mind while evaluating their worth: coverage, currency, and authority. How comprehensive is this information? Does it cover many aspects of the issue or just one or two? Determining currency (no, it doesn't have anything to do with money) means finding out how up-to-date the information is. Citing a study done in 1968 may not be the best evidence. Finally, how authoritative or trustworthy is your source? For example, if you cite a website, is it an official webpage (like the ones that end in .org, .edu, or .gov) or is it a website created by some guy sitting in his mother's basement? Look closely to see who published this site. Are they affiliated with any specific organization? If so, how reputable is it? Once you have gathered the information you will use, it's time to start putting it all together. Listed below are other helpful tips for completing research writing assignments successfully:

Researching Do's and Don'ts

1. Do choose a subject of interest that meets your class needs, and narrow it to a specific topic. Do preliminary research to discover your personal interests (unless the teacher predetermines the topic).
2. Do gather the needed research materials on your topic from a variety of sources that are both interesting and informative.
3. Do document useful sources while in the research process. Pay attention to where you found the title, author, and page number. This information will prove useful later.
4. Do categorize your notes into importance levels; this process may begin to take the form of an outline.
5. Do expound upon your ideas and outline.
6. Do add additional support material for your research.
7. Do compile a draft of your research writing assignment. This is usually a combination of your outline and research materials.
8. Do step away from your paper for a while and then reread it after some time has passed. You'll see things with a fresh eye.
9. Do allow your teacher, peers, or personnel in the Writing Center to give you constructive feedback.
10. Do edit for correct quotations, bibliographies and footnotes as needed until you have completed the final draft.
11. Don't underestimate your research writing capabilities. How can you go wrong with all this research to back you up?

12. Don't procrastinate. Pace yourself for best results.
13. Don't take feedback personally. It's an important part of the process.
14. Don't use boring, irrelevant, or outdated information.
15. Don't procrastinate. O.K., this is point 13 but it's worth repeating. (For a literary example of this dilemma, read Edgar Allan Poe's short story "The Imp of the Perverse.")

Theory into Practice: Research Papers

Below is an excerpt from Nick's research paper about the musical score of the movie Psycho. *Nick does a wonderful job citing his sources and writing a well planned and researched paper. In addition, Nick has paid particular attention to the rhetorical triangle; he realizes that his audience may not be knowledgeable about musical terms. This essay is a wonderful example of how to move from the library to the page.*

"Psycho: A Film Score Analysis"

Nick Melton

Bernard Herrmann (1911-1975) was perhaps the most talented musician to ever write for film, with hardly a single score that is not worth a look. Many of his works—*Vertigo, North by Northwest, The Day the Earth Stood Still, Taxi Driver, Citizen Kane,* and others—have defined and reshaped the sounds of specific genres of film music. Perhaps Herrmann's most famous score is *Psycho,* written for Alfred Hitchcock's suspense masterpiece. Scored for string orchestra, *Psycho* has withstood the test of time as one of Herrmann's most chilling and effective works. This paper will discuss why Herrmann's score works so well in the film and will then analyze two of the score's most important cues[1], "The Prelude" and "The Murder."

To truly understand the score to *Psycho,* one must first understand Herrmann's general style. First, Bernard Herrmann was not Max Steiner

---

[1] For definitions of musical terms, see Glossary.

(*Casablanca, King Kong, Gone With the Wind*) or Franz Waxman (*Sunset Boulevard, The Bride of Frankenstein, Rear Window*), who both employed the Wagnerian technique of "leitmotif," soaring and romantic themes for individual characters, events, or settings. Herrmann was much more fond of motifs, which are short rhythmic or melodic passages that are repeated or evoked in various parts of a composition. Therefore, one rarely encounters a massive theme in a Herrmann score. Secondly, Herrmann frequently practiced bizarre instrumentation, frequently augmenting and sometimes entirely removing sections of the orchestra. *The Day the Earth Stood Still,* for example, Herrmann orchestrated for thirty brass instruments, four pianos, four harps, electric violin, electric bass, high and low electric theremin, vibraphone, and pipe organ. *Beneath the 12-Mile Reef* contains a nine-person harp section and *Jason and The Argonauts* boasts expanded brass, percussion, and woodwind sections. It comes as no surprise, then, that *Psycho* contains only motifs and is scored only for strings.

This does not, however, mean that Herrmann scored *Psycho* for strings simply to experiment. Herrmann had a reason for everything he did. In regards to *Psycho's* instrumentation, Herrmann said, "I felt that I was able to complement the black and white photography of the film with a black and white sound" (Brown 111). This presented a problem, because as Fred Steiner pointed out, Herrmann's choice of orchestration

"deprived him of many tried and true musical formulas and effects which, until that time, had been considered essential for suspense-horror films: cymbal rolls, timpani throbs, muted horn strings, shrieking clarinets, ominous trombones, and dozens of other staples in Hollywood's bag of chilly, scary musical tricks." (Smith 237)

However, as Rimsky-Korsakov wrote, "Stringed instruments possess more ways of producing sound than any other orchestral group. They can pass, better than other instruments, from one shade of expression to another" (237). Herrmann was obviously aware of this and the resulting score was a masterpiece of mood and sound.

Herrmann's score works beautifully in the film for several reasons. One reason is that Herrmann frequently reprises material and techniques from the Prelude. "The real function of a main title, of course," Herrmann comments, "is to set the pulse of what is going to follow . . . I am firmly convinced, and so is Hitchcock, that after the main titles you must know something terrible must happen. The main title sequence tells you so" (Smith 238). In keeping with this philosophy, Herrmann uses the practice of ostinato established in the Prelude to build tension throughout the film. Early on, there is a scene in which Marion contemplates stealing $40,000 entrusted to her by her boss. The scene is two minutes long, contains no dialogue, and is relatively dull visually. However, the scene is incredibly tense, thanks to Herrmann's brooding ostinato. It is Herrmann's music that makes the scene.

GLOSSARY OF MUSICAL TERMS

Allegro (Molto agitato)—Fast and lively (Very agitated)

Bitonality—The use of two different keys, or tonic centers at the same time.

Chord—A set of notes, usually three or four, played simultaneously—usually containing a root, and other tones which have a tonal relationship to that root.

Chromatic—Motion by half steps; or pitches used outside of the diatonic scale in which they normally occur.

Coda—The concluding section at the end of a piece of music, not usually of structural necessity.

Cue—An individual musical fragment intended to be used in scoring a motion picture or TV/radio show episode. Cues can be used for underscore or for main titles, end titles, teasers, etc.

Con arco—Indication to play notes with the bow of a stringed instrument.

Diatonic—The notes that occur naturally in a scale, without being modified by accidentals other than in the key signature.

Ostinato—A persistently repeated musical figure or rhythm.

Pizzicato—Indication to pluck the notes on a bowed string instrument.

Prelude—An introductory movement or work.

Seventh—The interval of seven diatonic degrees.

Syncopation—Emphasis on the off-beat and a characteristic of jazz styles.

WORKS CITED

Brown, Royal. "Herrmann, Hitchcock, and the Music of the Irrational." *Alfred Hitchcock's Psycho: A Casebook*. Ed. Robert Kolker. New York: Oxford University Press, 2004. (101-117)

Psycho. Dir. Alfred Hitchcock. With Anthony Perkins and Janet Leigh. Universal Studios, 1960.

Smith, Steven C. *A Heart at Fire's Center: The Life and Music of Bernard Herrmann*. Los Angeles: University of California Press, 1991.

Wells, Amanda Sheahan. *Psycho*. London: York Press, 2001.

Surviving College Writing: Don't Be the First One Kicked Off the Island

Academic Integrity

Aaron Chandler

Academic Integrity: why have these two words appeared in every syllabus and student manual you've ever read? They've been repeated so often that it's hard to remember. Sure, you know it basically means "don't lie about your homework," or "you will be punished if you get caught doing so." What's hard to remember is that those two words are not primarily a threat, but a reminder of who you are when you become a student. Academic Integrity is a code that guarantees that your words, your efforts and your work belong to you. It is a bond of trust with your fellow students and your teachers. Without it, you cannot be given the trust and respect you deserve. Without it, your diploma would be worth about as much as yesterday's newspaper.

I know what you're thinking: big deal. It's a bond, it's a code, whatever. How's it going to help you get through semesters of writing papers and doing research? As it happens, it helps you quite a bit. Contrary to popular opinion, the code of Academic Integrity actually gives you the right to use other people's ideas for your own purposes, as long as you give credit where credit's due. You have the right to build on work that someone has spent decades compiling. You have the right to disagree with people who claim to be ultimate authorities. You have the right to ignore huge bodies of work if you think it has nothing to offer your project. Basically, you're in charge.

But that authority comes with some basic responsibilities. Be honest: don't pretend that someone else's words or thoughts are your own. Be fair: do not misrepresent your sources. Be respectful: treat the work and words of others the way you expect to be treated. If you don't keep up with these responsibilities, you force your teachers and peers into a position where they have to call you out as a person who is only pretending to be a student. Don't wind up in that spot. Ask your teachers how to cite properly, turn in your own work, and do not let others claim your words as their own because (and, yes, I know this is cheesy) your word is your bond.

The Writing Center
Liz Wilkinson

You've got a finished essay in front of you. It's good, but you want an A; you know that no matter how good this paper is right now, it could still be a little bit better.

Or . . .

You feel a cold sweat start to build. Your muscles are tense and your mouth is dry. Panic starts to well up in your chest and your heart is pounding. What's the cause of all this anxiety? You're sitting in English 101, your first college writing course, your instructor has just handed out the requirements for essay #1, and you're faced with the world's worst case of writer's block.

Or . . .

Your Poli Sci professor has assigned a research paper and requires that you use APA citations. You've got all of your sources and *think* you've got the APA format right, but you'd really like a trained eye to take another look at it with you.

The solution for all of these writing woes is a visit to the UNCG Writing Center. The Writing Center, located in 101 McIver, is staffed by trained undergraduate and graduate students who are happy to help with all sorts of writing challenges at all sorts of levels. You can call (334-3125) to make an appointment, or you can simply drop in with your essay and get one-on-one assistance with whatever writing issues concern you.

What happens during a Writing Center essay conference? You sign in at the front desk, and one of the staff takes you to a quiet corner where the two of you can concentrate on your paper. You'll start off by simply talking about the assignment, what you would like to accomplish during the conference, and your thoughts on the essay as it stands. Then, either you or the staff member will read your essay out loud. As the two of you are reading, the staff member will pause as needed to make suggestions, point out grammatical or punctuation difficulties, or address specific problems that you are concerned about. You can meet with a staff member at any stage in your writing process, from the initial idea to the last draft. The graduate and undergraduate students who staff the Writing Center provide a relaxed, safe, helpful place where you can discuss your writing without having to worry about being graded or judged.

Here's what a few students have said about their Writing Center experiences:

- "The Writing Center gave me great recommendations and helped me find problems I wouldn't have caught otherwise."
- "The people at WC are always very nice and they really know what they are doing. I never leave thinking I didn't get any help."
- "They are really helpful, but they don't tell you what to do. They allow you to make your own decisions with their help. They are really nice and seem to enjoy reading [. . .] papers."
- "It's a great way to sit and talk about your paper to make sure you are sending the right message through your writing."
- "It's worth making the time to go there."

Some things to remember/consider during a Writing Center conference include:

- Do bring a paper in any stage of development, even the initial brainstorming.
- Do come with plenty of time to work on the essay and with plenty of time to revise it after the session is over. Writing Center conferences can last about 30 minutes to an hour, depending on what you want to work on.
- Do be open to suggestions and expect to learn how to improve on your own writing and editing skills.
- Do bring the actual assignment instructions. This will allow the staff member to more accurately assist you.
- Do know that you can bring in essays, papers, or writing from any course, any time during your tenure as a UNCG student.
- Do expect your professor to be impressed that you took the extra time to visit the Writing Center.
- Don't expect that the staff will rewrite and edit your paper for you. Remember, above all else, this is *your* paper.
- Don't wait until the last minute. You won't have time to rewrite and/or edit, and it can be very frustrating for both you and the Writing Center staff.

❏ Don't be surprised if the Writing Center is *very* busy during midterms and finals. It's best to make an appointment during those times. You may also be limited to a one-hour session per day during those times of the semester, as well.

The Writing Center website, www.uncg.edu/eng/writingcenter, can provide you with a list of the staff and their hours, helpful links to on-line writing labs and workshops, links to MLA, APA, and AMA citation websites, and connections to other helpful services/centers here at UNCG. Have a great semester in English 101, and stop by the Writing Center as often as you would like. It is a free service provided by the university ready and waiting for you to utilize it.

> *One writes to make a home for oneself, on paper, in time, in others' minds.*
> —Alfred Kazin

Other UNCG English Courses

Writing Courses

101N ENGLISH COMPOSITION FOR NON-NATIVE SPEAKERS:
This course is for students who have learned English as a second language. Students will learn the basics of composition covered in other 101 classes, but in addition, the N sections will deal with specific concerns of non-native speakers.

102S ENGLISH COMPOSITION II, SPEAKING INTENSIVE:
English 102 builds on English 101 to help students continue to understand the principles of rhetoric through exploring the connections between speech and writing. Most sections are arranged around a theme. This course also helps students to become better speakers through group and individual presentations.

203 ACADEMIC ENGLISH FOR SPEAKERS OF OTHER LANGUAGES:
This course, like English 101N, is restricted to students whose first language is not English. It emphasizes the active use of language skills: speaking, listening, reading, writing. (It is **not** a replacement for English 101N).

219 JOURNALISM I: FUNDAMENTALS OF NEWSWRITING:
Students in this course get an introduction to newspaper journalism. There is an emphasis on basic newswriting and reporting. The course combines writing workshop and lecture.

221 WRITING OF POETRY:
English 221 is an introductory workshop in writing poetry. You must be at least a sophomore to take this course.

223 WRITING OF ESSAYS:
This is a course in reading and writing the essay, with particular attention to style and voice.

225 WRITING OF FICTION:
English 225 is an introductory workshop in writing fiction. It is only for students beyond the freshman year.

Introductory Literature Courses

104 APPROACHES TO LITERATURE:
This course will help students with critical reading and analysis of fiction, poetry and drama with an emphasis on a variety of major themes and their relevance to contemporary life.

105 INTRODUCTION TO NARRATIVE:
In English 105, students will do critical reading and analysis of American and British novels, short stories, and narrative poems. There is specific attention to historical, cultural, and literary backgrounds as appropriate.

106 INTRODUCTION TO POETRY:
This course focuses on the critical reading and analysis of British and American lyric, dramatic, and narrative poetry. There is attention given to historical, cultural, and literary backgrounds as appropriate.

107 INTRODUCTION TO DRAMA:
Students in English 107 will do critical reading and analysis of British and American drama. There will be attention given to historical, cultural, and literary backgrounds, especially the Continental dramatic background, as appropriate.

108 SPECIAL TOPICS BRITISH OR AMERICAN LITERATURE

109 INTRODUCTION TO SHAKESPEARE
This course introduces you to the wonder, beauty, and pleasure of Shakespeare's plays. Throughout the semester, you will read plays from the major genres (comedy, tragedy, history, and romance) as well as engaging in Shakespeare's sonnets. In addition, you will study Renaissance stage practices and language.

Campus and Web Resources

On-Campus Resources

WRITING CENTER
All students at all stages of the writing process are urged to take advantage of this free service.

www.uncg.edu/eng/writingcenter
101 McIver
334-3125

SPEAKING CENTER
Provides free assistance, feedback and counseling for students in speaking intensive classes. Please make an appointment in advance.

www.uncg.edu/~jedelk/index.htm
22 McIver
256-1346

COMPOSITION PROGRAM
Director of Composition
Elizabeth Chiseri-Strater
e_chiser@uncg.edu
www.uncg.edu/eng/comp/

OFFICE OF DISABILITY SERVICES
Students with any sort of disability who need accommodation for any of their courses should contact this office.

ods@uncg.edu
334-5440

LEARNING ASSISTANCE CENTER
Tutoring available for students who qualify.

success.uncg.edu/lac/
334-3878

COUNSELING AND TESTING CENTER
Students seeking counseling on academic or personal issues can contact this office for free services.

shs.dept.uncg.edu/ctcfrontpage.html
334-5874

STUDENT ACADEMIC SERVICES
Serves as a liaison between instructors and students in resolving academic and disciplinary issues.

web.uncg.edu/adv/
334-5730

UNIVERSITY TEACHING AND LEARNING CENTER (TLC)
Offers tutoring services, technical support, and holds the university's video library.

www.uncg.edu/tlc
334-5404

Web Resources

UNIVERSITY ACADEMIC INTEGRITY POLICY
Presents academic integrity policy, defines violations and outlines procedures.

saf.dept.uncg.edu/studiscp/Honor.html

Modern Language Association
This is the primary source for documentation in the English Department. You can also search the Modern Language Association data base via Jackson Library.

www.mla.org

Jackson Library
Whether you use Jackson library or go to the library website, this is a wonderful source for just about anything. The library employees are very helpful on-line, in line or at the front desk.

library.uncg.edu

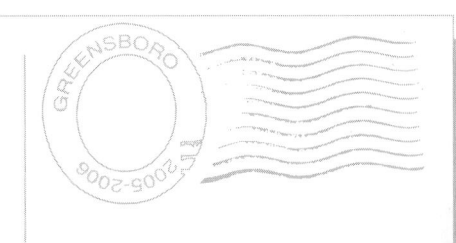

Contest Winners

In the Shadows

Katherine D. Frazier

When I was 5 years old I still prayed before I went to bed. Long before doubts of divinity or teenage cynicism I would kneel by my bed, hands dutifully folded, and chant without rhyme or reason, "Now I lay me down to sleep." On one of these nights as my father saw me off to bed he said to me, "Remember to pray for your Uncle Brad." I looked up at him, with small but wide and wondering eyes, "Why? What's wrong with him?"

As long as I can remember my uncle was in a wheelchair. His accident happened when I was only a few years old and all I know about it is through second-hand words. My grandfather insists there was something faulty with the breaks. My father admits that Brad was drunk. He has pointed out the tree on many occasions and described to me how they found him: the front of the car wrapped around the tree, my uncle unconscious. When I was much older my father confided in me that when he came to visit Brad in the hospital, he begged my father to pull the plug and let him die.

All the negative memories of Brad belong to other members of my family, I never saw him sad or upset; for most of my life I was kept from seeing him on the many occasions that he fell ill. As a quadriplegic he could not move his legs and the movement of his arms was very limited. He could feed himself because my grandmother had special silverware for him that would clasp around his hand, because his fingers would not bend, and he would clumsily lift the food up to his mouth then let his arm fall, as if exhausted.

He never seemed pitiful to me. The fact that he was in his thirties and needed someone to cut his food never seemed odd. The catheter bag attached to the side of his electric wheel chair, hidden in black, never seemed to be anything other than a convenience. When I was young, as far as I was concerned he lived the perfect lifestyle. His disability didn't occur to me as much as his eccentricities. He would get his son or my brother to put rubber snakes in the backpack attached to his chair, so he could scare the nurses at the home when he asked them to get something for him. On several occasions he was spotted going down the middle of busy roads in his wheelchair. He had no job, and even though his mother bought presents for him to give to us he would go to the dollar tree and pick something out for everyone. The last Christmas before he went missing he gave me his old thesaurus, wrapped in aluminum foil with a note attached. The note said "I bought this 8 years ago, but then I quit writing, this will do you more good than it does me." My uncle had written his whole life. In the months that passed afterward I would find treasure troves of his poetry, some of it absolutely horrible, and some of it breath-taking. Ever since I was young and expressed an interest in writing and art my Uncle had encouraged me. The thesaurus was yet another nudge toward writing, a passion we both shared. He also had an interest in seeing me act, but the small theatre I often performed at was not easily handicapped accessible.

When I was 17 years old I was working at The Stage Door Theatre in Fayetteville, just around the corner from Brad's Nursing home. On Friday nights I would come home late after we did two improv shows and closed out for the night. On one such night, when I called home, near midnight, to say I was on my way home my mother sounded worried. "Kati, your uncle Brad is missing. The nursing home said he left to go to a movie around three and never came back." She asked me to drive by just to look for him, to keep an eye out.

My heart was racing. A feeling of dread swept over me, but I convinced myself it was alright. My uncle had gone off on his own before and come back long after midnight, much to the chagrin of the nursing home staff. My mother hadn't reminded me of my uncle's recent medical troubles. My uncle had a tracheotomy ever since his accident. While it was no longer needed, the hole was kept as a convenience for when he had other medical problems. It had recently begun to build up scar tissue. Every four hours his trache had to be suctioned, otherwise he would basically choke on his own saliva.

I drove a few blocks out of my way and went by the nursing home, with its menacing gates. I looked into the small forested areas near by. My eyes began to deceive me: Was that Brad, or just a trash can? Is that my uncle behind the house, or just a shadow? A mailbox, a tree-stump in a wooded area all became the subjects of my paranoia.

With no luck in my search I drove home with a tight feeling in my chest. My family was still awake. They retold to me in detail how no one knew where he was; they listed all the people they had called looking for him: no one knew. I eventually went to sleep, against my better instincts. I woke shortly after sunrise, something unusual for me on a Saturday. My father had already left. My grandfather and he were out for another search for Brad. My mother began to talk about all her fears and doubts, and how she was sure he was already dead. These only made me feel worse and again my mind glanced upon the shadows and confusing shapes that had caught my eye the night before.

Sometime around lunch there was a phone call from my father. My uncle had been found. He was dead. He would not give details, he would not tell us where he was, he barely managed to get out those words.

Some hours later my father could clearly speak to me and he told me the exact circumstances. Between the nursing home and the nearby movie theatre there were several very small wooded areas where development hadn't occurred quite yet. One was a place where Brad and my father used to party in high school; perhaps he had gone there to reminisce. It was the same place where I thought my eyes deceived me the night before, where shadows and my own doubts had lead me to see what might have been a large stump or a trash-can, was my uncle. When they found him he had been dead for sometime; the tracks nearby lead them to believe he must have gotten stuck in the moist dirt. With a look of horror in his eyes my father told me that ants and other insects were crawling over his body.

The days that followed were a blur. I went to work at the theatre, thinking comedy would get my mind off of things. Aunts I had never met and cousins who I barely knew hugged me, kissed me, handed me platters of food and told me to bring them to my grandmother. My grandparents went from having nearly quit smoking (something my uncle had encouraged them to do), to smoking two or more packs a day. The newspaper published an article about my uncle and how he had inspired others which was full of anecdotes from my father and grandparents. The stories were all confused and jumbled; facts were wrong, and I tried so hard to tell people the real stories, ones that I hadn't even witnessed myself. My cousin, my uncle's son who lived with his mother, walked around in a daze, he spoke very little, he smoked very much. My mother was constantly swooping to his side and holding him, because no one else would.

At the "setting-up" I looked in the casket. It took a great deal of effort for me. At every funeral I had been to before I had refused to look at a dead body. The uncertainty had always plagued me. The idea that the person inside the wooden box was no longer a person, just a shell without a soul or thought, always frightened me. I went up after most people had looked so the line was gone. I walked to him quietly and looked down. His face was powdery and artificial, covered with makeup. He wore a suit that seemed so strange and foreign, as opposed to the army fatigues he liked to wear. In a moment of complete fear and surprisingly bravery I reached down and touched his skin with the back of my hand. The cold stiff feeling made me recoil instantly. Suddenly it was all too real. From the shadows in the woods came this: a cold foreign body. Guilt surged up in me till I felt I was going to vomit. I went outside where rain was sliding off the roof of the funeral home. There I found my cousin; we simply stood together and cried.

I wanted to say I was sorry. I wanted to say that I was a horrible person. That if I had simply told someone, that if I hadn't doubted myself so much his father might have had a chance. Instead I just put my arm around him.

At the funeral we sat in the front as part of the closest family. I felt horribly out of place in the church, as I am sure Brad would have. My uncle was a good person in the end, but not a religious man. When I was young, and Brad came to my Christmas pageants at church he always seemed antsy, with his attention moving from left to right; glancing at the foreign surroundings. Somehow the stained-glass windows seemed oppressive to him. The buttoned shirts and ties held him and the other men in restraints that seemed only visible to Brad.

A pastor who had never met Brad tried to tell stories about him, but again the facts were confused. Strangers and close relatives talked of my uncle like a martyr, as though he had no vice. They ignored how he drank too much. They all forgot how he stole from his parents as a teenager. Suddenly he was no longer a person. He became a sugar coated memory. The man they spoke of didn't seem to be related to me. The man they spoke of was not the Uncle I loved.

After the distant family left, and mourners who barely knew his name were gone my grandmother's house felt empty. She pulled out some boxes of my uncle's things and my father, my aunt, my cousins, and I were allowed to go through and take some things. My aunt tried to get her husband to take some shirts that might fit him. My brother took a chessboard, my father took a hat. My grandmother took a box of q-tips because she was almost out, and an unopened tube of toothpaste, for the same reason. I began to scavenge, angrily, desperately. I took an old 25 cent ring with duct tape around it, three bandanas (he would wear them around his neck to hide the patch over his trache), a hat with his name on the brim, and one of his army fatigue jackets.

I told no one about the shadows or about my guilt. To this day I have told no one in my family that there is a chance he could have lived, if I had only trusted my eyes.

About a month after Brad died, my car broke down on my way home from the Stage Door. I was about a block from my grandparents so I managed to coast to their house. There my grandfather looked under the hood and I called my father.

While I was there my grandmother gave me a box. It was a gift to me, from Brad. She said that they had found some presents for a few family members that he had bought, even though it was still four months till Christmas. The box was huge; my arms just barely wrapped around it to hold it. I couldn't help but wonder what could possibly be inside. But more than that I felt an overwhelming revulsion toward myself. I didn't want it. I didn't deserve it.

When my father picked me up and I got home I went to my bed room and closed the door behind me. I sat the box on my bed. I paced the room a bit, looking at the strange color and trying to decide: do I wait for Christmas or open it now? I opened it. I peeled away the yellow paper and the box underneath had no lid, instead there was a net of duct tape which I had to struggle with to peel off. Inside that was another box, and another, and another. Inside the smallest box was a large manilla envelope, folded up. Inside that was a small white envelope. Inside the small white envelope was a folded scrap of paper.

The paper read, "I.O.U." I cried for an hour, and when I thought I was done I got up and began to cry more.

When my car was fixed I drove to the graveyard. I solemnly walked up to the marble square that was my uncle's place in the outdoor mausoleum. My grandfather had placed fake flowers in the little vase attached to it. I knelt down before it. I folded my hands and leaned my head against the cold stone. Tears began streaming down my face and I did not pray. I just spoke. I apologized again and again. I said all the words I could not. I talked about how much I hated the reporter for ruining his story. I talked about how I hated my grandfather for giving him fake flowers when he deserved better. I talked about how I hated our family for talking about him like he was a saint instead of a man. I spoke of hate and guilt until there was nothing negative left in me. All that was left was the love I had for my uncle. I felt warm and quiet.

I plucked a fake petal from the fake flower at his grave. I took it home and placed it inside the thesaurus Brad had given me, between the same pages which held the I.O.U. I promised myself that I would go back again, and bring some real flowers and perhaps a poem or two. In my mind it was a sort of penance. That was over a year ago. I haven't been back to his grave since.

A Long Time Ago, in a Starbucks Far, Far Away...

Darrin Powell

As I drove down Hanes Mall Boulevard I anticipated what I would find when I entered Starbucks. The picture that came to mind was one of strong coffee aroma, light jazz or blues echoing in the background, and yuppie types sipping on espresso and discussing world peace. I arrived, found a parking space (which was difficult considering the lot was nearly full), and began my voyage into Starbucks.

The heavy aroma of coffee lingered in the air as I strolled in. I examined the scene that lay before me: eight tables, more chairs, bagged coffee for sale (naturally), coffeemakers for sale, mugs, 93.5 cleanliness rating, "Georgia on My Mind" by Ray Charles in the background. I made my way to the counter and saw that Yukon Blend and Fair Trade Blend were the two coffees being brewed. A sign was placed by the Fair Trade Blend on the menu that read "Temporarily Out." I was not in the mood for a fancy espresso based Frappuccino Cappuccino Chantico Yo-Mamma Latte, so I ordered a Venti (large) Yukon Blend and caramel pecan tart. I found a seat in the corner and sat and watched Starbucks unfold before my eyes.

Obi-Cheap Kenobi

As I sat at my table sipping my coffee and enjoying my pecan tart I noticed an older man at another table. He looked to be in his sixties, with grey hair, and glasses, neatly dressed, drinking a blended Frappuccino drink and totally engrossed in the sports section of The Winston-Salem Journal. I observed him for awhile; he was nearing the bottom of his drink, but he would not let that stop him. When he had extracted all the Frappuccino he could with the straw, he took the lid off, and turned the "plastic" glass up, mission accomplished. I now expected him to gather his newspaper, deposit his empty Frappuccino container in the garbage and exit the building, but, wait, he surprised me. Before he threw away his container and exited, both of which he did, he neatly put the newspaper back together, each section in order, folded it properly, and placed it back on the rack where the other Winston-Salem Journals *were for sale*. My question is why would a seemingly middle-class man not think twice about spending nearly three dollars on a fancy coffee drink, but will not shell out fifty cents for a newspaper? I do not know the answer, but maybe over the years he saved fifty cents here and there, and now he can afford the three dollar coffee.

R2D2 + C3PO = 4 TEENS

I then turned my attention to another table. This small round table was surrounded by four chairs each containing a bubbly, excited, smiling teenage girl. It was now approximately 2:45 PM, and school was over for the day; I suspected these four were classmates discussing their homework or possibly world peace. I noticed that each of them had her own drink, but they were sharing a caramel pecan tart, like mine. I listened a little closer, expecting to hear talk of the Pythagorean Theorem or the latest UN peace-keeping mission, but what did I hear discussion of? Boys; I was shocked! As I listened I realized these girls must be talking in some English dialect my forty year old ears have never heard. Individually their words made sense, but when they were put together I was lost. It seemed that one girl was doing most of the talking; the others were giggling and commenting occasionally. When they were finished the three gigglers left, while the lead conversationalist bought another coffee and then exited the building. I am sure they were off to discuss Geometry, world peace, and maybe boys.

It's So Cute; It Reminds Me of the Ewoks . . .

A man then came over and sat at the table next to mine; at first I did not pay him much attention; then a woman came over and joined him. She sat, said "hello" and commented she was late due to the "bad traffic." She then went to the front, ordered a coffee and returned to the table. Now I felt I was finally going to get something interesting; I was in an excellent position where I could hear the conversation, but still be inconspicuous. Maybe this was a "secret" rendezvous or a local crime syndicate planning its next job; I listened intently. The woman said she was having a "very productive day." They then began discussing their individual families; I learned they both have 17 month old babies: his a girl, hers a boy. He said he was having a "blast" with his child; he also described himself as "a big joker." The woman was not doing a lot of talking, as the man had taken control of the conversation. He went on to point out that he had been a Special Education teacher, but he was not spending enough time with his wife, who is 35, and his child so he was now doing this, whatever "this" is? I was now getting bored; when I woke up they were gone. My coffee must have been decaf.

Starbucks Episode 7: Revenge of the Barista

I could see that my time at Starbucks was nearing its end. The number of people was growing less and less, and my Yukon Blend was nearly gone. I thought about my expectations before I entered the Starbucks universe; yes there was a heavy coffee aroma, yes there was a jazzy/blues melody playing in the background, but the people were not what I had expected. It was a wide variety of persons, from the very young to the very old, from the peppiest of girls to the redneck boy on the farm. This did surprise me, and I thought as I rose to take my dish back to the counter, maybe the Starbucks universe is just as diverse as the larger world that surrounds it. As I placed my dish on the counter, the male barista asked me if I would like to try one of their new apple fritters; I said "no." He said "ok," but these fritters were the way he liked them; "crispy" he said. I replied, "Thanks, but no thanks," and exited the building.

I'm (the) Only Me

James Houghton

I woke up early. I could hear my mother in the kitchen, the salty smell of cooking bacon gathered in my nose. It was a special day! My father said grace without my noticing a single word he spoke. I droned "Amen" out of habit as he finished. I was too excited to care about thanking God for all the wonderful blessings I had been given. Why? Because it was Christmas!

I ate as much as my eight-year-old stomach could hold and then hurried off with my three brothers to wait until our parents said they were ready for us to open our presents. The four of us sat in the den, all wondering what could possibly be waiting for us in the living room. My father snapped the traditional picture of the shocked expressions on our faces as we saw the booty that had accumulated for us over the night. A new soccer ball, a Hotwheels set, and I screamed with joy when I saw "a new bike!" I know I had been told that it is "better to give than receive," but that aphorism was far from my mind that morning. I thought not of the toy I had bought my little brother, or how happy he had been to get it, but of how happy I was to have received a new bicycle. And that morning, in the shadow of my obese material gluttony, I forgot exactly what the gifts meant. I forgot exactly why the first six letters of Christmas were "Christ." I forgot to say thank-you for all the wonderful gifts I had been given. And I was disappointed. I didn't get a Nintendo, which was what I really wanted.

I cannot pinpoint the exact moment in time that my morals overthrew the materialistic dictatorship in charge of my perceptions of reality. Sometime during the past decade I must have gone through some type of enlightenment, a coup d'idéaux, an overthrow of my ideals, you might say—because now, I look ten years ago to that Christmas morning and see it through a completely different set of eyes. I will not claim to have achieved moral perfection, but time has given me the opportunity to legitimize the shortcomings of my past. In retrospect, my errors become obvious and I can forgive my childhood selfishness because at the time I was young and impressionable. I watched cartoons every Saturday morning and the commercials tortured me. The Nintendo seemed like the coolest toy a boy my age could conceivably own. There was a friend down the street who had a Nintendo, and I would often go to his house and play Ninja Turtles. I thought he was the luckiest guy in the world. I pleaded with my parents, everybody else has one. I need one, pleeeease!" But they got me a soccer ball and a bike. Had they even listened to me? I remember thinking they were mean and stingy for denying me this game system that was obviously the epitome of cool. Being that I was eight-years old, I can hardly call that shallow of me. Any young boy easily would be put to tears because his parents wouldn't purchase him this or that, while ignoring the fact that he is wearing clothes, eating food, and sleeping in a bed provided for by his "mean and stingy" parents. It is so easy to ask for too much, and so hard to accept what we get.

Still today I find myself struggling with temptation. But I think the most important lesson of my childhood comes from the reason I never got that Nintendo. It's ok to not have what "everyone else" has. And it's important that I not lose sight of that, especially if everyone else does. The lesson behind the Nintendo, whether intended or not, was that "it's ok to be different." One shouldn't need to "fit a mold" in order to "fit in," yet we use the term "fit in" to imply that adjustment is necessary for social acceptance. In order to "fit-in" at school, one must conform to the stereotypes of the clique they wish to hang out with; at least I have witnessed this. People are so concerned with the name on their clothes, the style of their hair, or the team they cheer for, that they lose sight of what really makes a person or a relationship.

It's amazing how many relationships are based off of material possessions like the shoes we wear, or the car we drive. We congregate based on the television shows we watch. People walk down the hallways at school singing the latest "hit" song. The box office charts tell us what movies we should be watching. Society sends the message that we should conform to ideals and items, and then share relationships based on our similarities. Hitler also thought it would be a good idea if everyone was the same.

People are so afraid of not being accepted that they'll abandon their own beliefs and morals to clothe themselves with society's brand-name personality. There are so many kids out there who want a Nintendo just because their friends have one. There are so many teens who smoke, drink, or are having sex because their friends either encourage them to do it, or worse, threaten not to accept them if they don't. Even adults find it hard to stand up for what they believe in, that's why when someone who does comes along, we admire them. Among these people are: Martin Luther King, Jr., Ghandi, Rosa Parks, and Jesus. It's no surprise that we look for relationships in people who are similar to us; we look for comfort in what we are familiar with. Our greatest fear is that we won't be accepted or loved. That is the driving force behind peer pressure. These are the temptations that have replaced my childhood desire to have a Nintendo: temptations to abandon who I am in order to earn an easy acceptance with the "in-crowd." It takes a lot of strength to preserve those things about me that are distinctly unique. It takes a lot of strength to be myself. But that's the strength Martin Luther King, Jr. encourages us to find: "If it falls your lot to be a street sweeper, sweep streets as Raphael painted pictures, sweep streets as Michelangelo carved marble, sweet streets as Beethoven composed music, or Shakespeare wrote poetry."

I stand on both sides of the fence: on one side, I'm admiring the lush green of the grass on the other side—I can easily give into temptation and change who I am to fit through the gate; on the other side I'm looking at someone and demanding that they alter something about themselves before I can let them into my field of friendship. It's so simple to look for similarities in those we meet, that we either ignore their differences, or see those differences as a bad thing. When human beings can't accept each other's differences we've got a big problem on the horizon. Just look at the Civil War, the Jim Crowe Laws, the Holocaust, the Red Scare, the wars between Palestinians and Israelis. People have been oppressed and murdered because they have different political ideals, different skin color, different religions, and different sexual orientations. I am the only one of me there is in this world. Were I, or any person, to forget this fact and give into the temptation of "fitting-in" against the grain of our morals, we'd be doing the world a great misfortune. No one looks at the big picture: "the world is a beautiful place and we all fit in just the way we are." If we continue thinking that compatibility comes from conformity, then we will never form the "big picture," because, like a puzzle, if all the pieces are the same shape, they will never fit together.

White Bullies

James Houghton

Hate crimes in America all spawn from the same motivator: the intolerance of diversity. Racial conflicts have historically been the most popular form of this intolerance. Race is not very hard to determine, which makes the victims of racial hate crimes easy targets for their aggressors. Obviously racial tension exists between America's ethnic groups, but why? Why are racist hate crimes occurring, and from where did this tension originate? The answer is that American society still reverberates to the beat of an old drum: Slavery.

America still tastes the bitter injustice of slavery. The English colonies of the 1500s and 1600s were the kitchen in which this miserable dish was prepared. The first Africans were introduced to Jamestown in 1619 as indentured servants. This group of blacks was no larger than twenty men, and to the English-speaking white men already settled in Virginia, these Africans were easily identifiable as different. The atmosphere was that of development; however, Virginia, at this time, still paid taxes to England. The most important aspect of settlement life was agriculture, harvesting the supplies to pay the English Parliament. The terrain of Virginia was much different from that in England and nurtured the important cash crop of tobacco.

In the beginning, everyone worked the tobacco fields, whites and black alike (Jordan 31). Historian Winthrop Jordan guesses that the Negro's status never matched that of the white servants', but certainly any racial equality, if it ever existed, did not last for a very long time. Jordan claims that the Africans were "treated as somehow deserving a life and status radically different from English and other European settlers" (Jordan 26). He continues to show that this separation perpetuated a cycle of Negro debasement. Soon the Africans had drifted from indentured servitude to slavery. The white landlords eventually took all liberty away from the blacks, and with this loss of liberty came a loss of humanity (Jordan 31).

The slave masters legitimized the bondage of the African people by equating blacks with "infidels and heathens" (Jordan 32). The white men were constantly on the lookout for anything to keep control over the black race. "[The Planters] charged themselves with supplying for the needs of society and regulating the lives of its members and expecting deference and obedience in return" (Parent 200). This idea that slavery was morally justified as an asset to society parallels the Mafia's neighborhood watch concept. While in both cases the white slave owner and the Mafia claim to be protecting society from heathens, the real instigator to this front of so-called moral righteousness is power. The slave owners simply wanted to back their claim for power with a valid explanation.

The concept of a "patriarchal society" first appeared in 1666. Patriarchalism was a "society . . . structured around the supremacy of the patriarch, or father" (Parent, 199). This gave white men an immense amount of power. With that great power came indisputability; the white man's word was final. Slave owners maintained authority by twisting facts for legitimate reasoning; having derived power through what seemed like justifiable means, the slave owner earned the trust and respect of the white race. Meanwhile, "Africans in America were . . . powerless" (Jordan 50).

It was the "raw power of . . . the enslavers" that ensured the control over the "enslaved blacks . . . . The threat of violence kept their slaves in check" (Parent, 198). Blacks were constantly whipped and abused by their masters. The slaves lived in inhuman conditions and supplied their owners with grueling workloads every day. It did not take long for the slaves to realize that they were obviously not receiving fair treatment. The first protests to the oppression of slavery were the runaways. Lathan Windley compiled a three volume set of Runaway Slave Advertisements. Each volume is over 1,000 pages thick with anywhere from six to twenty advertisements per page. From 1730 to 1790 there were hundreds of thousands of runaway slaves. This fact in addition to the vague descriptions of some dark-skinned African worth a reward if returned had whites on the lookout for any free black man. The advertisements had no intention to catch any one specific runaway slave, but to keep the entire race in check by wielding this threat above the heads of the blacks: You might not have escaped yet, but because you are black, we are already looking for you.

Over three-hundred years later, the societal influence of slavery still looms large in our modern culture. Over the centuries of American development the white man has used bullying to keep on the top of the social hierarchy. He sits there now, contented with his supremacy, claiming to be understanding but still dodges controversy with twisted reasoning. There are claims that race relations are improving, yet race is still the greatest instigator of hate crimes from a 2002 statistical survey put out by the FBI. Fifty percent of the bias-motivated offenses are race related, and of those there are four times as many anti-black crimes than there are anti-white. More than 50% of all racially motivated hate crimes are anti-black. Anti-black hate crimes are flowing from a pump primed with slavery. There are whites today who still can't tolerate the equality of a black man. It was slavery that initiated the intolerance to diversity. It was slavery that said, "If you look different, you get treated differently." It was the slave owners that started the reasoning for white supremacy that many racists still use today.

The year was 1900. Avery Mills and his wife, Raney, were "new Negroes"—born outside of slavery. They were tenant farmers in the town of Forest City, North Carolina, for the rich, white landowner, Mills Flack. The stories have it that Flack approached Raney one morning inquiring over a bushel of peaches to which he, as proprietor, believed himself entitled. Raney did not believe that Flack deserved the fruit and a heated argument ensued. The argument was ended when Flack left upon the alleged threat placed upon his life by Raney Mills' pistol.

Raney Mills broke the "unwritten code of racial etiquette . . . [that] all whites, regardless of individual merit, [had to] be accorded the deference due to members of the superior, ruling race" (Cole 63-64). Flack had been refused the fragile respect that two centuries of black oppression had afforded him. The next morning he returned again to the Mills' farm with a loaded shot gun. Flack, accompanied by his son Otho and one of his son's friends, was stopped on the outskirts of the property by Avery Mills who confronted him for having argued with his wife the previous day. This, too, became an aggressive quarrel eventually leading to Mills throwing a rock at Flack; and as a white man, Flack knew no way to react to black contempt but with violence (Cole 64). Flack fired his shot gun, striking Mills in the hip. Some sources claim that Mills already had a pistol on his person, while others say that he called for it and Raney brought it to him. No matter which source is true the effect of either circumstance is the same. Mills H. Flack was shot by Avery Mills and died but an hour later.

The word of mouth and the newspapers circulated the murder; however, the papers initially printed false witness to who shot first and what the circumstances of the aggression were. The malicious descriptions of Avery Mills as a "black beast," along with the missing fact that Flack fired the first shot fueled the racial passions of the whites. "A mob bent on vengeance is moved by emotion, not reason," and the white mob that formed within 24 hours of the incident was most definitely moved by anger to avenge the death of Flack (Cole 67). Mills Flack's dying breaths were used to request that his friends find and kill Avery Mills. The police wagon carrying Avery and Raney Mills to Rutherfordton was over taken by a mob of 250 white men from Forest City. The Police refused to turn Avery over to the mob at which point the mob removed him from the wagon. Insisting that Mills was to be taken on to jail, the Sheriff approached the men. The mob acted in haste and shot Mills 20 times then abandoned the dead body to make their escape into the woods.

The Charlotte Daily Observer headlined that day, August 29, 1900, that Mills had been "lynched at noon . . . shot by a mob." In analysis, the article claimed that the initial conflict started when Mills shot Flack and then tried to shoot Flack's son. The article not only claimed that it was Mills who fired first but also tainted his moral and ethical humanity. The article read that "Mills H. Flack was 60 years of age and a Christian and a worthy citizen" while "the negro Mills had a bad record." The reason why Avery Mills was lynched is not because he simply shot Mills Flack, but because Mills was a "negro with a bad record" and Flack was "a worthy, white, Christian citizen."

Had another white man shot Flack, or had Mills killed another black man there would have been no such uprising to put the murderer to justice. But it was a black man who killed a white man, and the size of the mob shows the unanimous communal outrage of the whites. The Black man has a place on the bottom of the hierarchy, and the Whites belong on top. It was white supremacy that murdered Avery Mills. White supremacy punished him for refusing to tolerate being treated as a subhuman. White supremacy made sure that Avery was not seen as a beacon of hope, a brave black man who had stood up against the white machine of tyranny, but as a measly black man who had been put in his place: six feet under. Mills Flack and Avery Mills were both buried on the same day, the same depth under the same dirt on the same planet.

The Forest City lynching represents an early example of a racial hate crime born from the ideals of slavery. Slavery polarized society—reserving the top for only the white males and subjecting everyone else to one degree of debasement or another. Under the rule of a master, the slave faced immediate repercussions for stepping out of line (whipping, branding, mutilation, etc.). Using fear as a lever, the whites were able to lift themselves to a position of power and control above the blacks. While the blacks lived under the fear of the whip the whites also lived in fear: that the black man might come to question his power.

Whites bullied their way to becoming the dominant race. How do you spot a bully? Linda Starr gives a few research proven facts about bullies: bullies are looking for control, victims are chosen because they are weak and unable to retaliate, bullies justify their behavior. It has often been said that the victims of bullying often have feelings of inadequacy that generate a tendency to depression. Other victims have been shown to become violent and aggressive themselves. Look at the first white slave owners.

Were they looking for control? Yes. Were their victims weak and unable to retaliate? Yes, in 1649 blacks made up only 2% of the population in Virginia and the threats of violence kept them from retaliating (Jordan 40). Did the bullies justify their behavior? Whites referred to slaves as "infidels and heathens" (Jordan 32). Being Christian came to mean that you were white, and the slave owners used this to claim that God supported them (Jordan 51). Look at the victim race. Have they suffered depression or responded in violence? In the 1995 FBI report on hate crimes, 27% of the crimes had a black offender. A speech made by Cynthia McKinney demands reparations,

> *not only for the transatlantic slave trade, but also for the Jim Crow trains and the segregated buses, for the poll taxes and the white primaries, for 100 years of lynching, and the white water fountains . . . For all the blacks who are disproportionate—disproportionately in the military, disproportionately poor, disproportionately sick or unemployed, or underemployed, or undereducated . . . For all the targeted black men who have been shut up or shut down merely because they dared to speak about black power. (McKinney)*

Blacks still feel the burden put on their race by the whites. Affirmative action programs are the result of the disadvantage that the African American race has been subjected to by the Anglo-Saxons.

Since the Emancipation Proclamation of 1863, black men and women have lived with the depression of ubiquitous segregation, the Jim Crowe South, discrimination, racial profiling, unfair hiring practices, unequal job pay. Our society is still reeling from the effects of hate. Martin Luther King Jr. claimed that he'd stick with love because "hate is too great a burden to bear." Hate is solid and suppressive, like a stone slung over one's shoulders, hence the image King creates of hate as a burden. Unfortunately, that stone of hatred was the cornerstone upon which our whole country was built—the foundation for a temple of white supremacy. Our society has long since cast that stone into the pool of justice but is still rippling from the memory of the hate that America's forefathers carried for so long. It was over a century ago that bullets of hatred pierced the body of Avery Mills, and while most whites have now learned the lessons of love preached by Martin Luther King Jr., still not everyone has seen the light. The tragic irony of this is that King himself was assassinated by a white man who feared the effects that a message of equality might have on the American white dictatorship. This is the humbling truth of our daunting past: America will live in the shadow of slavery until every man, woman, and child kindles the light of love in their own heart and the hearts of their neighbors.

WORKS CITED

"Black Peoples of America: Slave Punishments." History on the Net. 23 Oct 2004 <www.historyonthenet.com/Slave_Trade/punishments.htm>.

Cole, Timothy J. *The Forest City Lynching of 1900.* Jefferson: McFarland & Co., Inc., Publishers, 2003.

"Hate Crime 1995." Federal Bureau of Investigation: Criminal Justice Services Division. FBI. 20 Oct 2004 <http://www.fbi.gov/ucr/cius_02/html/web/offreported/02-nhatecrime12.html>.

Jordan, Winthrop D. *The White Man's Burden.* New York: Oxford University Press, 1974.

Maggio, Michael, ed. *Quotations for a Man's Soul.* Paramus: Prentice Hall Press, 1998.

McKinney, Cynthia. "We Demand Reparations." 23 Oct 2004 <http://www.blackcommentator.com/64/64_reparations_mckinney.html>

"Of Bullies and the Bullied." *Psychology Today.* 23 Oct 2004 <http://cms.psychologytoday.com/articles/pto-19930101-000010.html>.

Parent, Anthony S. *Foul Means: the Formation of a Slave Society in Virginia, 1660-1740.* Jackson: University of N.C. Press, 2003.

Starr, Linda. "Sticks and Stones and Names Can Hurt You: De-Mythtifying the Classroom Bully!." 7 Nov 2000. School Issues Article. Education World. 23 Oct 2004 <http://www.education-world.com/a_issues/issues102.shtml>.

Windley, Lathan A., ed. *Runaway Slave Advertisements.* 1st ed. Westport: Greenwood Press, 1983.

Writing Matters Submission Form

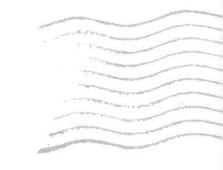

Writing Matters is looking for new student writing for future editions. If you have a piece of writing that you did for English 101 that you'd like to submit, please fill out the form below completely and include (1) your writing printed out, (2) a copy of your writing on disk, and (3) a description of the writing assignment. Please do not submit originals; your submissions will not be returned to you. You may give it to your English 101 instructor or put all the required pieces in an envelope labeled "Writing Matters" and take it to the English Department, 132A McIver.

PLEASE PRINT CLEARLY.
(You may photocopy this form as needed):

Name: _____

School Address: _____

Permanent Address: _____

Local Phone: _____

Permanent Phone: _____

Email: _____

Title of Writing: _____

English 101 Instructor: _____

RELEASE
I hereby grant *Writing Matters* permission to use my piece in a future edition. The editors have my permission to edit or abridge the piece to fit their needs.

Signed: _____